AIR VANGUARD 9

SUKHOI Su-25 FROGFOOT

ALEXANDER MLADENOV

First published in Great Britain in 2013 by Osprey Publishing, Midland House,
West Way, Botley, Oxford, OX2 0PH, 43-01 21st Street, Suite 220B,
Long Island City, NY 11101, USA E-mail: info@ospreypublishing.com

Osprey Publishing is part of the Osprey Group

A CIP catalogue record for this book is available from the British Library

Print ISBN: 978 1 78200 359 5
PDF ebook ISBN: 978 1 4728 0478 5
ePub ebook ISBN: 978 1 4728 0479 2

Index by Fionbar Lyons
Typeset in Deca Sans and Sabon
Originated by PDQ Media, Bungay, UK
Printed in China through Asia Pacific Offset Limited

13 14 15 16 17 10 9 8 7 6 5 4 3 2 1

Osprey Publishing is supporting the Woodland Trust, the UK's leading
woodland conservation charity, by funding the dedication of trees.

www.ospreypublishing.com

CONTENTS

INTRODUCTION   4

DESIGN AND DEVELOPMENT   5
- The need for a dedicated attack jet
- Flight testing effort
- Production plant for the Su-25
- Target-towing Su-25BM

TECHNICAL SPECIFICATIONS   18
- Fuselage
- Wings and undercarriage
- Flight controls
- Airframe systems
- Cockpit
- Engine
- Fuel system
- Combat survivability features
- Navigation, attack and communication equipment
- Ordnance

Su-25 VERSIONS, MODIFICATIONS AND PROJECTS   28
- Su-25K for export customers
- Two-seater Frogfoots
- Su-25UTG for carrier landing training
- Never-built versions
- Su-25T Super Frogfoot
- All-weather Su-25TM
- Su-25SM – the RuAF's current upgrade standard
- Su-25K Scorpion
- Su-25UB for SEAD
- Su-25M1/UBM1 upgrade in Ukraine

OPERATIONAL HISTORY   43
- Afghanistan
- The Frogfoot in the post-Soviet wars
- Export Frogfoots in combat

CONCLUSION   63

FURTHER READING   63

INDEX   64

SUKHOI Su-25 FROGFOOT

INTRODUCTION

Ugly, sturdy and hauling heavy bombloads, the Sukhoi Su-25 (NATO reporting name Frogfoot) made its maiden flight in February 1975 and was the first Soviet mass-produced combat jet purposely designed for the close air support (CAS) role. As such, it represented a simple, effective and survivable attack workhorse. In its original guise, the Frogfoot was designed to fly short-range and low-level battlefield CAS missions and, in the 1980s and 1990s, proved itself a powerful and cost-effective weapon doing this rather dangerous job.

The Frogfoot received its baptism of fire just five years after its maiden flight. It was Operation *Romb* in Afghanistan in 1980, during which the field evaluation and testing effort of the new aircraft was carried out in so-called 'peculiar conditions' – as real-world war conditions have been referred to in the official Sukhoi Design Bureau and Soviet Air Force documentation. It was considered an integral part of the type's extensive and rapidly progressing state testing and evaluation programme. Since then, the faithful Frogfoot has seen use in anger in a good many local conflicts worldwide and is likely to see further combat employments in the near- and mid-term.

The legendary Il-2 Shturmovik and its improved derivative Il-10, seen here, proved effective mass-produced attack aircraft, widely used for low-level battlefield CAS and anti-tank missions by the Soviet Air Force during World War II. (AERO Bulgarian Aerospace Magazine archive)

The true and firmly successful jet-powered successor of the prop-driven World War II-era Ilyushin Il-2 and Il-10 Shturmovik model line was eventually developed on the basis of the dissatisfactory lessons learned from the use of the Sukhoi Su-7B Fitter-A, the first-generation purpose-designed supersonic fighter-bomber type fielded in the Soviet Union. Furthermore, numerous exercises and local conflicts – such as these in the Middle East and Vietnam in the late 1960s – clearly demonstrated that a new-generation tactical strike aircraft, well protected and capable of delivering heavy warloads, was required. The new machine was set to replace both the subsonic and obsolete MiG-17s, which had been re-rolled as fighter-bombers, and the supersonic and still rather new Sukhoi Su-7Bs and Mikoyan MiG-21s. The latter two jets were forming the backbone of the Soviet Air Force's tactical strike force at the time, but both proved disappointingly ineffective in the low-level tactical ground attack role.

It was something of a surprise for the Soviet military leadership that, during exercise *Berzina* in 1969, the hopelessly obsolete MiG-17 Fresco performed much better than its supersonic Su-7B Fitter and MiG-21 Fishbed counterparts, hitting all the assigned ground targets. This somewhat strange occurrence was explained by the MiG-17's lower manoeuvring speed of 270–324kt (500–600km/h), which, in turn, provided notably better conditions for target recognition and sighting before unleashing rockets or releasing bombs. The same conclusions were drawn from the attack operations in the 1967–70 War of Attrition between Egypt and Israel, where the faithful Fresco once again demonstrated far better weapon delivery results and recorded fewer combat losses than the more modern and far more speedy Fitter-A when employed by the Egyptian Air Force for attacking well-protected Israeli targets beyond the Suez Canal.

In the Soviet Union, the military leadership was largely disappointed with the Su-7B's performance from the very beginning and, as a consequence, ceased ordering any new production batches by 1967. New types of fighter-bombers and attack aircraft were clearly needed to re-equip the VVS's tactical strike force in the 1970s.

DESIGN AND DEVELOPMENT

The need for a dedicated attack jet

Despite its huge experience in fielding dedicated heavily armoured low-level attack aircraft for the CAS and anti-tank roles during World War II – in the form of the legendary Shturmovik Ilyushin Il-2 and its improved derivative Il-10 – the Soviet war machine abandoned this niche business shortly following the beginning of the jet era. As a consequence, no such aircraft were procured for the VVS (Voyenno-Vozdushniye Sily, the Soviet Air Force) battlefield strike assets until the early 1970s.

In fact, in the late 1940s and early 1950s, the Ilyushin Design Bureau undertook a number of private-venture attempts to keep alive the Shturmovik theme by developing a well-armoured and heavily armed jet-powered Il-2/10 successor for low-level CAS operations over the battlefield. Designated as the Il-40, the new machine made its maiden flight in March 1953 and was recommended for serial production in 1954, but, two years later, the programme was abruptly cancelled and subsequently the two prototypes, used in the flight test effort, as well as five completed pre-series airframes, were scrapped.

The initial mock-up of the new jet-powered attack aircraft proposed in the early 1970s by the Sukhoi Design Bureau – known as Kulon Machine-Building Plant at the time – was considerably smaller, with less combat load and armour protection than the definitive Frogfoot, as developed in the second half of the decade. (Sukhoi Company)

A team of forward-thinking designers at Sukhoi Design Bureau – then officially known as Kulon Machine-Building Plant and led by chief designers Oleg Samoilovich and Yuri Ivashetchkin – began some conceptual preliminary design works during March 1968, based on the idea proposed by Ivan Savtchenko, a teacher at the Soviet Air Force Academy at the time, named after Yuri Gagarin. He taught frontal aviation combat employment tactics and was the first expert to formulate a set of specific requirements for a new-generation affordable CAS jet. On their own initiative, the members of this informal design team outlined the concept of an all-new, 8-tonne-class, twin-engine light attack aircraft. From the outset, it was to feature extensive composite armour protection – using layers of steel and aluminium plates, separated by a rubber layer – and up to 2 tonnes of ordnance. Tentatively named Light Army Attack Aircraft, the conceptual attack machine was to be powered by a pair of Ivchenko AI-25T turbojet engines, each developing 17.2kN (3,865lb st) of thrust. The project received the internal Sukhoi Design Bureau designation T8 and, later on, upon entering VVS regiment service, the official designation Su-25 was adopted.

In August 1968, the preliminary project was presented to various command levels of the Soviet military establishment, but all replied that the air force did not need such a class of dedicated ground attack and CAS jet. Design bureau founder and head, Pavel Osipovich Sukhoi, however, decided to continue with the project as a private initiative by building a wooden mock-up, which was completed in September 1968. It is of note that, during World War II, he began his career as head of an aircraft design bureau with the development of specialized attack aircraft. This is why Pavel Osipovich Sukhoi saw the project as his moral duty and his mission to facilitate the renaissance of the Soviet Air Force's attack aviation branch in the jet era.

Sukhoi's patience, persistence and confidence in the viability of the T8 project eventually paid off as, in late March 1969, the Soviet Ministry of Aviation Industry forwarded to his design bureau a request for proposal for a new-generation jet-powered attack aircraft that was required to meet a set of VVS specifications, approved earlier in the same month. This request for proposal was, in fact, an announcement of the formal tender for the development of such a new class of jet-powered combat aircraft; the other competitors being the design bureaux of Mikoyan, Yakovlev and Ilyushin.

The Su-25's sole competitor in the VVS programme for fielding a new-generation Shturmovik in the late 1970s and 1980s was Ilyushin's Il-42, later re-designated the Il-102. It was a much larger two-seat dedicated attack aircraft with a heavier warload, rear gunner and rather austere sighting equipment outfit. (Author's collection)

The technical specification, drawn by the VVS, called for a jet with a combat manoeuvring speed between 270 and 520kt (500 and 800km/h), normal payload of 2,200lb (1,000kg), maximum payload of 6,600lb (3,000kg) and range at ground level of 404nm (750km). It was to be capable of employing free-fall bombs – weighing between 220 and 1,100lb (100 and 500kg) – and rockets of between 57mm and 240mm calibre. In addition, the future attack aircraft was required to be a cost-effective solution, i.e. simple, affordable and easy to produce and maintain, and, last but not least, to boast a high degree of combat survivability.

The Sukhoi attack aircraft concept was further developed in comparison with the version originally conceived, as the AI-25T engines were replaced by the more powerful Mikulin RD-9, a non-afterburning version of the turbojet powering the Mikoyan MiG-19 and Yak-27R. This provided a much higher thrust-to-weight ratio in order to satisfy the speed and manoeuvrability performance requirements. The project successfully passed the first phase of the tender and was shortlisted for the second phase, competing against the proposal of Mikoyan Design Bureau, designated the MiG-21LSh. Yakovlev was rejected at the first phase of proposal, calling for the development of an armoured derivative of the Yak-25 twin-engine fighter – designated the Yak-25LSh – while the Ilyushin proposal called for an improved derivative of

The T8-1 prototype was considerably different to the production standard, with notably shorter fuselage, fin, wings and the distinctive VPU-22 ventral gun pack, housing a twin-barrel GSh-23 23mm cannon. (Sukhoi Company)

its 1950s-vintage Il-40. It received the new designation Il-42 (later re-designated the Il-102) and lacked any sophisticated targeting equipment, but had a dedicated gunner for rear hemisphere protection as featured on the World War II-era Il-2/Il-10 Shturmovik.

Before submitting the project for the second phase of the competition, the Sukhoi Design Bureau took into consideration a good many recommendations provided by pilots with rich ground attack experience. The most important of these called for installing the targeting suite borrowed from the Su-17M2 Fitter-D fighter-bomber, and increasing the warload up to 6,614lb (3,000kg). During the evaluation stage of the tender in August 1971, the speed performance of the aircraft turned out to be the bone of contention as Sukhoi was ready to offer a maximum speed at ground level of 485kt (900km/h), while the competing Mikoyan proposal – based on the MiG-21 Fishbed fighter – promised 647kt (1,200km/h).

In the event, the Sukhoi project was declared the winner in the competition against the Mikoyan's light attack aircraft design (the Mikoyan Design Bureau eventually decided not to continue its further participation in the tender becauuse of various internal reasons) in 1971, but there was no funding allocated by the Ministry of Aviation Industry for commencing any follow-on development works for the project. In this unfavourable situation, Pavel Osipovich Sukhoi took the bold decision in late 1972 to proceed with the manufacture of the first T8 prototype without government approval, using only the company's internal funds, re-directed from other programmes running within the design bureau.

At the same time, the VVS representatives continued to insist that the new attack aircraft have a higher maximum speed than that proposed by the design bureau – no less than 647kt (1,200km/h) when carrying four B-8M rocket pods. The maximum speed proposed by the design bureau, however, was constrained to 485kt (900km/h), and such limitation was set in a bid to avoid using hydraulic boosters in the aircraft control system, keeping it as simple as possible. The dispute over the maximum speed issue between the VVS and the design team continued for several years and, in the event, the parties reached a compromise in November 1971 by agreeing to 540kt (1,000km/h), translating into Mach 0.82 at low level. As the chief designer Oleg Samoilovich recalled, this compromise has caused numerous subsequent design and development troubles. The agreed flight range was 404kt (750km) and the take-off run was 1,500 to 1,800ft (500 to 600m) when operating from unpaved runways.

The first T8 prototype was assembled in deep secrecy at the design bureau's experimental plant in Moscow and, when completed, it was unofficially presented in April 1974 in front of the Minister of the Aviation Industry, Piotr Dementiev. He had an immediate liking for the T8 and put his weighty support behind the bureau's design and development efforts, offering to make official the construction of two prototypes of the new aircraft. The respective formal resolution of the ministry, which officially referred to the T8 as test-experimental aircraft, was issued in early May 1974, but then the VVS abruptly intervened in the process, insisting the two T8 prototypes be reworked in a bid to meet the service's formal tactical and technical requirements. This rework was eventually carried out within an extremely compressed timeframe; as a result, the first prototype – designated the T8-1 – was completed by the end of 1974 and declared ready for commencement of ground and flight testing. The article that was intended for static testing – wearing the T8-0 designation –

was completed in late August 1974; by the end of the year the preliminary results of its static testing allowed the Sukhoi Design Bureau to issue a permit for the commencement of the T8-1's flight testing programme. The full static testing cycle of the T8-0 article was successfully completed in January 1976.

Flight testing effort

The T8-1 prototype was completed in October 1974 and in November it underwent a series of engine runs and checks of the electrical and air condition systems at Sukhoi's experimental plant in Moscow. The aircraft was then ferried by road to the company flight test station at Zhukvskii airfield near Moscow on 23 November for a series of follow-on ground tests, including high-speed taxi runs, as it was slated to make its maiden flight by the end of the year. This, however, proved impossible on account of some unexpected technical difficulties and the maiden flight was consequently postponed to 13 January 1975. This target date was also missed as, during an engine test run the morning before the flight, the starboard engine suffered a turbine bearing failure with the separation of several turbine blades that went through the engine nacelle, causing a small fire. Fortunately this fire was immediately extinguished by the technicians and the T8-1 suffered minor damage only. In mid-February, it was promptly repaired and received an improved pair of R9-300 engines. After a successful high-speed taxi run, performed on 21 February 1975, the T8-1 at last made its maiden flight the following day, 22 February, in the capable hands of the Sukhoi Design Bureau's famous chief test pilot, Vladimir Ilyushin.

T8-1's first flight testing phase – the so-called factory testing effort undertaken by Sukhoi – lasted from the second half of February until November 1975. Its chief purpose was to explore the main performance data, stability and controllability of flight, as well as the powerplant improvements. In general, the initial flight test results met the expectations of the design team, though the antiquated and rather thirsty engines reduced range below the VVS requirements and extended the length of the take-off run from unpaved runways. In addition, the line maintenance of the new aircraft proved to be a complex and lengthy undertaking, while test pilots tended to complain that the stick control forces were excessively high – especially for bank control – and that the lack of airbrakes made speed control in dive rather difficult.

The T8-2D reworked prototype is seen here in 1976, sporting a rather heavy warload of eight UB-32-57 32-round packs for 57mm rockets and a pair of R-3S heat-seeking air-to-air missiles for self defence. (Sukhoi Company)

In June 1975, the new aircraft was deployed to the Soviet Air Force's Flight Test Centre at Akhtubinsk in an effort to evaluate the engine stability performance when employing the aircraft's built-in gun and rockets. It was discovered that the S-5 and S-8 rockets – fired from 32- and 20-round packs respectively – were not causing any disturbances, while the considerably larger and heavier S-24 and S-25 proved far more problematic as they tended to cause a sharp rise in turbine temperature, resulting in engine surges.

The T8 flight test report, issued in late November, following completion of the testing and evaluation phase, confirmed that the new aircraft possessed wide-ranging capabilities for attacking ground and air targets and sported good controllability, allowing it to be flown by student pilots who had just completed their basic flying training phase, i.e. admitting that the T8 was also suitable for use in advanced and weapons employment training roles.

This report also noted that the way of enhancing the T8-1's overall combat capabilities – in order to match the VVS requirements – required the introduction of a new engine, sporting maximum thrust of between 7,700 and 8,800lb st (3,500 and 4,000kgf) and lower specific fuel consumption than that of the rather antiquated R9-300.

Between November 1975 and January 1976, the T8-1 underwent an additional series of flight tests, in an effort to explore its capabilities in operating from snow-covered unpaved runways. The results showed that the aircraft could safely take off from and land on runways covered with up to 10in (25cm) of unpacked snow.

The second flight test prototype – designated the T8-2 – introduced a plethora of design improvements, such as airbrakes on engine nacelles, a built-in stairway, a K-36L ejection seat, an all-new design canopy and an improved air conditioning system, as well as a taller, increased-area fin to improve the directional stability. The T8-2 took the air for the first time on 26 December 1976, again piloted by Vladimir Ilyushin. It was used for flight testing of wing strength characteristics, as well as for evaluation of airbrake effectiveness and bank control design improvements. In the summer of 1977, the T8-2 was involved in a further series of weapon trials in order to evaluate the engine stability performance during firings of various types of missiles and the built-in 23mm cannon in the VPU-22 gun station, housed in a pronounced gondola fairing below the starboard lower fuselage.

The decree of the Ministry of Aviation Industry for launching the serial production, issued on 7 June 1976, also required the T8 to receive a new and more powerful engine. There were, however, no new-generation, fuel-efficient turbofan engines in an acceptable state of readiness in the Soviet Union to allow installation on the T8 at the time; as a consequence the design team had to make a selection from among the few existing turbojet options. One of the alternatives then under consideration called for developing an increased-thrust R9-300 derivative, rated at 8,360lb st (3,800kgf), but even this rating was not enough to provide the required performance enhancements. In the summer of 1976, a suitable powerplant alternative cropped up, calling for the introduction of a non-afterburning derivative of the tried Tumanskii R13-300 turbojet from the MiG-21 fighter. This engine, designated the R-95Sh and produced at the engine-building plant in Ufa, weighed 2,178lb (990kg) and was rated at 9,020lb st (4,100kgf/40,22kN). A 1950s-vintage technology, the R-95Sh, had relatively high fuel consumption but was otherwise known as an extremely robust and reliable design. Among the unique features of this engine was its ability to run using different non-standard types of fuels, including vehicle diesel fuel, limited to four hours of operation.

Production plant for the Su-25

At the time the T8 series production finally commenced, the Sukhoi Design Bureau suddenly encountered new and rather serious difficulties, as there were no production plants willing to engage with the manufacture of this rather unorthodox attack aircraft. The traditional producers of all previous Sukhoi combat aircraft types – the factories at Komsomolsk on Amur and Novosibirsk – promptly rejected the proposal to commit to the production of the new attack aircraft; the same negative reply was also received from the factories at Ulan-Ude, Smolensk and Irkutsk. In the event, the only facility that expressed willingness to engage with the Su-25 was the Tbilisi Aviation Production Plant in Tbilisi, Georgia, then known as Aviation Plant No. 31, named after Georgy Dimitrov. At that time it was completing the production run of the MiG-21UM two-seater and had just commenced manufacture of the new R-60 (AA-8 Aphid) short-range air-to-air missile. A decree, issued by the Soviet Council of Ministers on 7 June 1976, ordered launching the Su-25 into production at the Tbilisi-based plant. Another decree, dated 29 June 1976, also insisted on the acceleration of the Su-25's development programme and the introduction of a series of further design improvements to the existing two prototypes. In their new guises, the T8-1 and T8-2 were required to be submitted for the state testing and evaluation effort in spring 1978 and to complete this stage by the autumn of 1980.

The new Soviet attack aircraft type was detected at Zhukovskii for the first time by a passing US intelligence satellite in 1977, and was allocated the provisional reporting name 'Ram-J', indicating that it was the tenth new aircraft type spotted at the main Soviet flight test base, then known in the West as Ramenskoye.

In early 1976, the T8-1 prototype was redesigned and received a good many new modifications, such as new airbrakes, while a yaw damper was also added to improve in-flight stability. In October 1976, after logging 172 sorties, the T8-1 underwent another series of further extensive modifications, including re-engining with the R-95Sh turbojet, in order to be brought to configuration close to the definitive production standard. The T8-2 was also re-engined and received a host of modifications already planned for implementation onto the T8-1; under the new designation T8-2D, it took the air for the first time on 7 December 1976. During the flight tests, the tailplane installation was changed from 5° anhedral to 5° dihedral, and the engine installation axis was angled downwards and outwards at 2° in order to prevent interaction between the engine jet blast and the tailplane that was causing unwelcome buffeting.

The T8-4 prototype – the second Frogfoot built at the Tbilisi plant – took the air for the first time in September 1979 and was used to support the flight test and evaluation effort until 1984, when it was handed over to the Moscow Aviation Institute to be employed as ground instructional airframe. (Sukhoi Company)

One of the main issues reported during the flight test, namely the unacceptably high stick forces in pitch and bank channels, was partially resolved thanks to the introduction of mechanical servo-compensator devices, borrowed from the Cessna A-37B. One ex-South Vietnamese A-37B was delivered to the Soviet Union in 1976 and its design was studied in detail. The compact servo compensators – used to reduce the stick forces of the A-37B – featured a smart design using torsion springs, which was promptly copied for use on the Su-25. The new design feature was flight tested for the first time on the T8-2D in mid-1977.

The reworked T8-2D prototype completed its factory test phase by November 1977 and, up to 1980, saw use in a number of specific test programmes for the improved control system and the new powerplant, as well as for the improved anti-surge engine protection during rocket firings.

In May 1977, the Sukhoi Design Bureau presented the representative production version of the T8. The definitive Su-25 featured a lengthened fuselage, increased-span wings and taller fin, as well as the new R-95Sh turbojets in enlarged nacelles that were provided with new air intakes, an armoured bathtub for the pilot – welded titanium plates with thickness between 10 and 24mm – and a new VPU-17A gun pack with a built-in GSh-30 (AO-17) 30mm twin-barrelled cannon. The new aircraft also received the proven targeting system and navigation aids, integrated on the Su-17M3 Fitter-H swing-wing fighter-bomber.

The rework of both the T8 prototypes to the definitive production standard proved to be a protracted undertaking, with the first of them, the T8-1D, being completed within 18 months. In April 1978 it was handed over to the VVS for commencement of the type's joint state testing effort – the so-called Stage A of testing and evaluation – carried out by the VVS with the support of Sukhoi (in 1977, the company saw change of its formal name from Kulon Machine-building Plant to Sukhoi Machine-building Plant).

T8-1D took to the air for the first time in its new guise on 21 June 1978, with Vladimir Ilyushin behind the controls. The first flight showed that the new increased-span wings reduced the critical Mach number from 0.82 to 0.75, as the new design was prone to so-called 'Mach buffeting' at high speeds.

The first T8, produced at the serial plant at Tbilisi, was completed in the summer of 1978. Designated the T8-3 (c/n 01001), this example featured an entirely new assembly technology for the lower wing panels and, as such, was

1. The T8-4 prototype c/n 01002 was used as the production-standard specimen. Built in Tbilisi, it was flown for the first time on 19 September 1979 and was employed for all controllability and stability tests and evaluation trials, as well as in various performance-defining trials and spin characteristics testing.
2. The Soviet Air Force Su-25s used in the last years of the war in Afghanistan introduced a comprehensive set of combat survivability enhancements, in order to be made capable of withstanding hits from the Stinger hand-held SAM. The aircraft wore three-tone camouflage, with its belly and a significant proportion of the sides painted in light blue.
3. After the break-up of the Soviet Union, the newly established Belarusian air arm inherited a fleet of 19 two-seaters, but now only a few remain in service, as most of the Frogfoot-Bs were sold out in the late 1990s and early 2000s. Known export sales include eight to Peru, two to the Ivory Coast and one to Macedonia (via Ukraine). This aircraft belongs to the 206th Attack Brigade in Lida.
4. Iran's Islamic Revolutionary Guards aviation service took on strength three newly built Su-25UBKs in 2004 and, thus far, these are the last-known newly built Frogfoots exported by Russia. The Frogfoot fleet was reinforced in the mid-2000s by seven ex-Iraqi Su-25Ks that fled to Iran in January 1991.

limited to manoeuvring loadings of up to 5G; it also introduced production-standard targeting equipment and navigation aids. The T8-3's manufacturing and assembly quality, however, proved to be very poor, and the production quality at Aviation Plant No. 31 in Tbilisi continued to be a serious issue, evident on all the Su-25s assembled there in the 1980s and early 1990s. The T8-3 eventually became the production-standard specimen for the type and took to the air for the first time on 19 September 1979, again in the capable hands of Vladimir Ilyushin.

The T8-4 was the second pre-production example that rolled off the line in Tbilisi in 1979, while in 1980 two further examples – designated the T8-5 and T8-6 – followed suit.

Stage A of the type's joint state testing and evaluation effort was completed on 30 May 1980, and the final VVS report noted that the aircraft and its systems had been found to be in working condition, demonstrating the required specifications of technical, flight and combat employment. The scope of the definition of these characteristics in the T8 during Stage A was judged sufficient to proceed with the more comprehensive Stage B of the type's joint state testing and evaluation effort.

Even before the completion of Stage A, it was decided that the type should be tested in real-world combat conditions in Afghanistan; in fact, it was an initiative promoted by the Minister of Defence, Dmitrii Ustinov. Two aircraft, the T8-1D and the T8-3, were promptly modified and deployed to Shindand airfield in Afghanistan to undergo the demanding combat employment testing phase. Both were limited to 485kt (900km/h) maximum speed and manoeuvring at up to 5G.

The test and evaluation campaign in Afghanistan, code-named Operation *Romb*, lasted for 50 days and brought valuable results, proving that the Su-25 could fight effectively in the CAS role. It was also found that the new aircraft was considerably more effective than all other Soviet jets used for CAS in the Afghanistan war theatre. As many as 100 sorties were logged, with a total flight time of 98 hours and 11 minutes, including 44 combat missions.

Stage B of the type's joint state testing and evaluation effort commenced on 18 June 1980, utilizing both the aircraft that had just returned from Afghanistan and the third pre-production example, the T8-5. The testing effort experienced a serous setback as the T8-5 was lost on 23 June; the cause of the crash was wing disintegration as the test pilot pulled 7.5G during manoeuvring, despite the aircraft being limited to 5G only. Sukhoi pilot A. Yegorov was killed during the disintegration. The root cause of the crash was never discovered, though, according to the chief designer, Oleg Samoilovich, a manufacturing defect in the elevator's servo compensator device could be viewed as the most likely cause for the T8-5's loss.

Between July and December 1980, Stage B continued using the three available aircraft – the T8-1D, T8-3 and T8-4 – for defining the aircraft's performance during combat employment sorties. Another aircraft, the T8-6, joined the effort in August 1980 and was used for trials and evaluation of the 30mm built-in cannon. These trials showed that the R-95Sh engine

The T8-3 prototype saw the end of its life in a series of combat damage resistance trials (i.e. to test the titanium bathtub for the pilot), having cannons of up to 40mm calibre fired at the cockpit sides from close ranges at Lubertsi range near Moscow. (Sukhoi Company)

had some serious stability issues during gun-firing runs and thus stringent restrictions were imposed on the throttle movement, with the engines being required to be set at idle rating for no fewer than six seconds before pressing the trigger in a firing run. The T8-6 was also employed for trials of the engines running on diesel fuel, performing as many as eight sorties in the course of this test phase.

The T8's entire joint state testing and evaluation effort, which undertook as many as 186 sorties, was successfully completed by 30 December 1980. The only remarks in the VVS's final test programme report referred to the small number of aircraft used in the effort that, in turn, did not allow evaluation of the full scope of the type's spinning characteristics or complete the gun-firing trials of the GSh-30 built-in cannon. There were no other significant remarks in this final report and, as a result, the type was recommended to be launched into serial production.

The formal commissioning of the T8 into VVS service, however, was delayed until fixing of all the shortcomings reported during the test and evaluation programme had been completed, and it therefore took place seven years later; the commissioning order of the Soviet Minister of Defence is dated 18 April 1987. As many as ten Su-25 production series, representing specific production standards, rolled off the line at Aviation Plant No. 31 in Tbilisi between 1978 and 1990, totalling no fewer than 812 aircraft, including 180 built for export customers.

After completion of the joint state testing and evaluation effort, the T8 prototypes and some of the pre-production aircraft continued to be used in the course of various trials programmes. One, the T8-1D, was subsequently lost in flight on 21 January 1981, when the VVS test pilot, A. Ivanov, exceeded the maximum allowable Mach number during a bombing dive run; the aircraft was asymmetrically loaded with bombs and rolled upside down while still in dive. The pilot realized that the aircraft could not be recovered into level flight due to the excessively high stick forces, and he eventually decided to eject from 1,980ft (600m). After this incident, the Su-25 received an Angle Of Attack (AOA) limiter and a new set of operational limitations was imposed with regard to the carriage of asymmetrical loads.

In 1982, the T8-4 was involved in a series of trials from a ski jump, under a programme for developing a carrier-capable T8 derivative. Upon completion of these trials, the aircraft was transferred to the Moscow Aviation Institute to be used as a ground instructional airframe. The T8-3, in turn, saw use in a series of battle damage resistance trials at the range of the Research Institute on Aircraft Repair and Operation at Lubertsi near Moscow, where it was fired at from close range, using different types of weapons, in order to evaluate the effectiveness of the type's combat survivability features.

There were some other early production aircraft involved in various trials, such as the T8-9 used for spinning trials, while the T8-10 saw use in take-off and landing trials from snow-covered and unpaved runways with different weapon loads. At a later stage, this specific aircraft was also used for trials of the Kh-25ML and

This Su-25, used as ground instructional airframe in the Perm Military Aviation Technical School, was among the aircraft built to the so-called 1st Series production standard that rolled off at the plant in Tbilisi in 1980 and 1981. (Andrey Zinchuk collection)

Kh-29L laser-guided air-to-surface missiles, as well as testing of backward-firing B-8M 80mm rocket packs and SPPU-22-01 gun pods. The trials of the back-firing ordnance – undertaken by the VVS Flight Test Institute in Akhtubinsk in the early 1980s – were considered successful, but the project underwent no further developments and was eventually abandoned.

The T8-11 was the first of the type to feature hydraulically actuated ailerons, with non-reversible boosters borrowed from the MiG-21 fighter.

These Frogfoots are seen at the flight line of the Soviet and then Russian Air Force Flight Test Centre at Akhtubinsk, used in trials of various natures and also for training of military test pilots. (Andrey Zinchuk collection)

This solution provided a significant improvement in the controllability in bank and, as a consequence, the maximum permitted speed increased up to 540kt (1,000km/h). The T8-11 was also utilized for airframe strength testing in order to increase the maximum permitted manoeuvring loads up to 6.5G. Another set of improvements – tested on the T8-11 – included the new and more effective airbrake W-shaped design, with four separate moving sections and the wingtip anti-glare plates for the retractable landing lights, as well as the KMG-U bomblet/mine dispensers. This hard-working aircraft saw further trials with engines running on diesel fuel and special radar-absorbent coatings; the latter were a result of the so-called Astra research programme, which saw graphite coatings applied to the wing leading edges and the tail surfaces. The T8-11 was also involved in other, vaguely exotic trials, such as new paint rendering to make the aircraft's visual detection more difficult and trials for the deployment of nuclear free-fall bombs.

Another pre-series aircraft, the T8-12, saw trials with the L203 Gardenya-1FU response jammer pod system.

Target-towing Su-25BM

Both the T8-14 and T8-15 were built as production-standard Su-25s, subsequently modified for trials of the new and more powerful R-195 engine, intended for use on the new Su-25 derivatives. This engine was a follow-on development of the R-95Sh with increased rating, and its IR signature was significantly reduced thanks to the introduction of extended jetpipes pumping fresh air – taken from air scoops to the rear nacelle – into the hot jet efflux. The improved engine also boasted improved resistance to surges, caused by powder gases ingestion during gun-firings and large-calibre rocket launches.

The T8-15 was also utilized to test an additional bank of ASO-2V-01 chaff/flare dispensers installed on the engine nacelles, as well as for the newly added RSDN-10 long-range aid to navigation and the Gardenya family of jammer pods.

The first of these new Su-25 derivatives, powered by the new R-195 turbojet, was the Su-25BM, a dedicated target-tug and target-launch aircraft that retained the full combat capability of the original Frogfoot. The Su-25BM's full-scale development began in 1988 and the flight testing of the first aircraft, modified from a standard Su-25 – taken from the 10th Series (c/n 10489) and designated the T8BM-1 – commenced on 22 March 1990. In addition, the T8-15 also joined the trials, used as a launch platform for the PM-6 diving target.

The Su-25BM was an improved derivative of the basic Frogfoot-A, with increased-thrust engines and a better navigation system in order to be employed in the target-towing and target-launching role, but after dissolution of the Soviet Union the 50-strong fleet – built in 1990 – was employed by the Russian Air Force (RuAF) as ordinary attack aircraft. (Andrey Zinchuk collection)

In September 1990, the T8BM-1 commenced the trials of the TL-70 podded winch system with the Kometa towed target; due to difficulties encountered during the factory test effort, it was not completed before October 1991. The VVS test and evaluation effort for the TL-70 then followed, lasting from October 1992 to January 1993.

The Kometa target was towed on a 9,900ft (3,000m) cable behind the Su-25BM and was equipped with the Planer miss distance indicator. It was carried in a pod under the port wing, while on the starboard wing a counterbalance was carried in the form of a FAB-250 or FAB-500 bomb. The winch of the towed target was controlled by a panel installed in place of the ASP-17BTs-8 reflector sight, while the miss-distance results were downlinked in real time to a ground receiver station; the electronic boxes of the miss-distance indicator and the downlink were housed in a small underfuselage pod.

The avionics of the target-towing Frogfoot were expanded with the integration of the RSDN-10 long-range aid to navigation, used for precise positioning (required for the launch of the PM-6 dive targets); it also received the new A-325 tactical aid to navigation, which replaced the obsolete RSBN-6 system.

As many as 50 Su-25BMs rolled off the line at the Tbilisi plant in 1990, within the scope of the 10th Series production standard, and the first of them wore construction number 10503. These target-towing Frogfoots were handed over to the Soviet Air Force – the first of them going to the 186th IShAP (instructor attack regiment) stationed at Buturlinovka, as well as to 34th OBAE and 65th OBAE, independent target-towing squadrons stationed in Novorossia in the Far East and Damgarten in Germany – as well as to the 80th OShAP (independent attack regiment) in Sital-Chai. In fact, both the target-towing equipment and the target itself were never delivered, as the TL-70 podded winch was to be manufactured by the Tbilisi plant and the Kometa in Ukraine. Understandably, the procurement of both systems proved impossible after the dissolution of the Soviet Union. In the event, the Su-25BMs were used as highly priced attack assets thanks to their powerful engines and considerably better navigation system.

The TL-70 Kometa podded winch and towed target system was purposely developed for use by the Su-25BM. Carried on the port centre wing pylon, it was counterbalanced by a FAB-500M-62 bomb suspended on the opposite wing. (Andrey Zinchuk collection)

TECHNICAL SPECIFICATIONS

Fuselage

The Su-25 featured semi-monocoque, riveted, slab-sided fuselage with an all-welded titanium-armoured cockpit, monolith panels forming integral fuselage tanks and a number of armour plates protecting all the important systems onboard. The main construction materials used in the airframe comprised aluminium alloys (some 60 per cent), steel alloys (19 per cent), titanium alloys (13.5 per cent), magnesium alloys (2 per cent) and other materials (5.5 per cent).

The fuselage was manufactured in three principal sections. The forward section, located between frames 0 and 12, included unpressurized nose bays, housing the navigation and targeting equipment boxes (provided with four upward-opening access doors), unpressurized cockpit with the gun station bay beneath it, and the nosewheel bay and rear avionics bay situated just behind the cockpit. The nose tip incorporated a downward-opening forward fairing to provide access to the Klyon-PS laser rangefinder and target designator equipment boxes.

The centre section, located between frames 11b and 21, included the built-in centre-wing section, the enclosed fuel tanks 1 and 2, the non-variable air intakes, the engine air ducts, the main undercarriage wheel bays and the spine.

The rear section was located between frames 21 and 35, and included the non-detachable engine nacelles, the non-detachable horizontal stabilizers and the tail cone housing the twin-dome brake chute.

The main pitot system was installed onto the boom protruding from the starboard side of nose, which was also used to support the fixed antennas of the RSBN-6S tactical aid to navigation, while the port boom housed a back-up pitot system.

Wings and undercarriage

The shoulder-mounted and modestly tapered straight wings had a high aspect ratio and featured a dogtooth leading edge (on the outer 50 per cent of each wing) and dedicated tip pods. Each wing was swept at 19° 54', had a 2° 30' anhedral from the roots and thickness/chord ratio of 10.5 per cent. The total wing area was 362.75 sq ft (33.7 m²) and loading was 106.5lb/sq ft (520kg/m²) at the maximum take-off weight.

The main load-bearing members of each wing were designed in the form of a torsion box, contained between spars 1 and 2 and ribs 1 and 10. The five hardpoints for carrying the weapon load were attached to ribs 3, 5, 7, 9 and 11 of each wing.

Each of the wings was provided with five-section leading-edge slats across the full span (deflecting at 12° for landing and 6° for manoeuvring on the single-seater), two-section double-slotted trailing-edge flaps (deflecting at 40° for the inner and 35° for the outer section for landing, and 10° for manoeuvring on the single-seater) and ailerons (deflecting at 20° up and down).

The wingtip pods each split at the rear to act as W-shape (also known as crocodile-type) airbrakes and were 13sq ft (1.2m²) in area, projecting below and above pod when extended. Deflection of each hydraulically operated main airbrake section was 55°. Each pod housed a PRF-4M retractable landing light with glare shield and the forward-facing antennas of the SPO-15LM Beryoza radar warning receiver (RWR).

The undercarriage was hydraulically retractable and of tricycle type. Mainwheels retracted to lie horizontally at the bottom of the engine air-intake trunks. Each main undercarriage member was provided with a single KT-163D wheel with a low-pressure tyre on a cash-levered suspension unit, with oleo-pneumatic shock absorber, while the nosewheel was of the KT-21 type. Mainwheel tyre size was 860x360 and pressure was 135lb/sq in (9.30 bars), while nosewheel size was 660x200 and pressure was 106lb/sq in (7.35 bars). The mainwheels had hydraulic brakes with antiskid units. The forward-retracing, hydraulically steerable nose member was installed offset to port, and its wheel was provided with a mudguard/debris deflector.

The Su-25 was the first mass-produced jet in the former Soviet Union purposely designed for the Close Air Support (CAS) role. It was provided with a well-armoured cockpit and windscreen and powered by an old-fashioned yet highly reliable powerplant borrowed from the MiG-21. (Author)

The aircraft had a PTK-25 twin-dome cruciform brake chute with a total area of 272sq ft (25m^2), housed in the tailcone and normally released after touchdown. In case of rejected take-off, the brake chute was stressed for use at speeds up to 124kt (230km/h).

Flight controls

Flight controls were conventional and partly assisted, with only the ailerons, the full-span slats and the double-slotted flaps hydraulically actuated. The ailerons used the BU-45 irreversible boosters and were also provided with manual backup and had multiple tabs. The elevators and the two-section inset rudder were manually operated. Each elevator and the lower rudder segment were provided with tabs. The upper rudder also operated as an automatic yaw damper.

Elevators deflection was +23° to –17°, while rudder deflection was 25° left and right. The variable-incidence tailplane had 19° 54' sweptback and 5° dihedral, and was provided with three positions: –1°, –3° 12' and –7° 56' respectively. This allowed the aircraft's balancing to be eased and provided enough elevator authority for all flight regimes.

Airframe systems

The electrical system was 28V DC, supplied by two engine-driven AC generators and two batteries. There were two DC generators (supplying 28.5V power) and two AC generators (36V/400 Hz), and a pair of DC converters.

The aircraft featured dual independent engine-driven hydraulic systems (main and backup), used to operate the undercarriage, slats and flaps, ailerons, tail incidence, airbrakes, main wheel brakes and nosewheel. Systems ran at a pressure of 2,987lb/sq in (206 bars).

The air conditioning system took bled air from the eighth stage of the compressor, which then passed through two heat exchangers and a turbocooler. It was used to supply fresh air to the cockpit in order to maintain a degree of overpressure to prevent NBC contamination. In addition, air was supplied to the pilot's anti-G suit, ventilated the windshield and canopy, and also cooled the avionics compartments.

The oxygen system was used to supply an air-oxygen mixture to the pilot's oxygen mask at altitudes in excess of 6,600ft (2,000m), while above 23,000ft (7,000m) only pure oxygen was provided. The gaseous oxygen was contained under pressure in four 5l bottles housed in the nosewheel bay. The K-36L ejection seat housed an emergency oxygen bottle intended for use in the event of high-altitude ejection or when problems with the main oxygen system were encountered.

The fire extinguishing system included the SSP-2I fire warning sub-system and the UBSh-4-2 fire extinguisher sub-system, installed in the engine bays and divided into two manually controlled stages. The two fire extinguishers were filled with Freon 114 V2 inert gas at 65 per cent volume, while the remainder was occupied by pressurized air. The number of extinguishers was later increased to six.

Cockpit

The Su-25 featured a conventional cockpit in layout, very similar to that of the Su-17M3, with rows of key conventional round 'steam gauges' instruments, switches and selectors. The entire cockpit was painted in a blue-grey colour and pilots tended to comment that it was roomy, comfortable and ergonomically laid out; they also noted that the Frogfoot cockpit was generally much better than that of the MiG-21 and MiG-23/27.

The starboard side console and cockpit wall held the navigation system, the radio, the transponder, lighting and chaff/flare dispenser controls, as well as the engine start panel and generator controls. The rail-mounted throttles were fixed on a pair of parallel rods on the port cockpit wall. The port console also held external stores, weapon selectors and jettison controls. In addition, the trimmers drag chute, oxygen and air conditioning system controls were housed there.

The cockpit was provided with a Zvezda K-36L ejection seat with zero altitude and 54kt (100km/h) forward speed limitation. It was a lightened and simplified version of the K-36D – as used on the MiG-29 and Su-27 fighter – but without the leg and arm restraints required for high-speed ejections.

The canopy featured a rear-view mirror on top and was hinged to starboard; there were additional rear-view mirrors on both sides of the windscreen frame. The aircraft was provided with a folding ladder for access to the cockpit built into the port fuselage.

The classical 1970s-vintage cockpit of the Frogfoot was filled with steam-gauge instruments. This one belongs to an Su-25K that was modified in the 2000s with the add-on of stand-alone TACAN, VOR and ILS receivers. (Author)

The old-fashioned but remarkably reliable Soyuz/Gavrilov R-95Sh non-afterburning turbojet, rated at 8,800lb (4,000kgf/41kN), was used to power the vast majority of the Su-25s in Russia and around the world. (Author)

Powerplant R-95 turbojet	
Length	2700mm
Diameter	772mm
Dry weight	1,815lb (825kg)
Maximum continuous thrust rating	8,800lb (4,000kgf or 39.24kN)
Emergency thrust rating	9,020lb (4,100kgf or 40.22kN)
Alternate powerplant R-195 turbojet	
Length	2700mm
Diameter	772mm
Dry weight	1,881lb (855kg)
Maximum continuous thrust rating	9,460lb (4,300kgf or 42.18kN)
Emergency thrust rating	9,900lb (4,500kgf or 44.14kN)

Engine

The Su-25 was powered by two Soyuz/Gavrilov R-95Sh turbojet engines, installed in nacelles in wingroots, with a 5mm-thick firewall between them. The R-95Sh, built in the Ufa Engine-Building Plant, was a twin-spool turbojet with an axial compressor, annual combustor, axial turbine and non-variable nozzle. The axial compressor featured three-stage low-pressure and five-stage high-pressure sections, while the annual combustor featured ten combustion chambers, each provided with twin igniters, and the axial turbine had two stages. An auxiliary gearbox was mounted on the base of each engine, housing generators and hydraulic, oil and fuel pumps.

Both the R-95Sh and its improved derivative R-195 were made to be capable of running on all known types of kerosene and even on diesel fuel, limited to four hours with regard to the latter.

Fuel system

The fuel system included tanks 1 and 2 in fuselage, holding a total of 2,385l, and a pair of wing tanks, designated tank 3, each holding 637.5l. The tanks were filled through an open and centralized gravity filler cap, located on fuselage tank 1. The total internal fuel load was 6,614lb (3,000kg) on the single-seater and 6,608lb (2,725kg) on the twin-seater. There was also provision for four

PTB-800 800l drop tanks, carried on underwing pylons 3, 5, 7 and 9. PTB-1050 drop tanks – each holding 1,053l – were also cleared for use by the Su-25 in Russia, but these were routinely used only by the Russian Navy Su-25UTGs on long-range ferry flights. In addition, 1,500l drop tanks were known to have been cleared for use by the Su-25Ks sold by Georgia to Democratic Republic of Congo in 1999–2000 and also by the Su-25/UBs sold by Belarus to Peru in 1998.

Combat survivability features

The self-defence aids of the basic Su-25 included a SPO-15L or SPO-15LM RWR and up to eight ASO-2VM (ASO-2V-01 on the early production machines) chaff/flare dispenser units – each containing 32 26mm PPI-26 IR countermeasure flares or chaff cartridges – mounted on the rear upper fuselage at the tailfin sides and above the rear engine nacelles. There was also provision for the SPS-141MVG Gvozdika active radar jamming pod, carried on wing pylon 10.

The Su-25's airframe was designed with a very robust structure and provided with extensive system redundancy in an effort to achieve sufficient

PRINCIPAL COMBAT SURVIVABILITY FEATURES

• A full armour 'bath' for the pilot made from welded titanium alloy plates (with a thickness between 10 and 24mm) and capable of withstanding hits by up to 50 20mm or 23mm projectiles without cracking.
• Damage-resistant load-bearing members used in the fuselage structure.
• Widely separated engines – at 5ft (1.5m) from each other – with a 5mm stainless steel screen installed between them in order to prevent simultaneous damage of both engines from a single missile warhead detonation or a high-speed projectile hit, and also to prevent fire from one engine progressing to the other.
• Large-diameter pushrods (up to 40mm) instead of cables were used as control runs for actuation of the flight control surfaces, in order to provide a high level of redundancy and hardening in case of mechanical battle damages or in-flight fires. The pushrods were capable of withstanding hits by 12.7mm bullets. The pushrods for the elevators were made dual-redundant and the control runs were widely separated. In 1986, new steel pushrods with increased resistance to fire were introduced, replacing the original titanium-made design.
• Fuel tanks were filled with reticulated polyurethane foam (occupying some 70% of the tank volume) for explosive wave and fire suppression and were lined with twin-layer thick porous resin protectors (with 20mm thickness) for protection against the explosion of the kerosene vapours and to prevent large leaks when punctured by projectiles or high-speed fragments.
• All the basic items of equipment and fuel system components were armour protected. The enhanced protection package, introduced in mid-1987, included 17mm of titanium plating under the belly to protect the fuel lines that fed the engines, as well as a 17mm-thick titanium plate installed onto the starboard engine cowling to protect the oil tank and its pump control unit. The ASO-2V chaff/flare dispenser units next to the fin also received 5mm armour screens to protect against high-speed missile warhead fragments. The 10th Series Su-25s also received an additional 18mm of aluminium alloy armour plates scabbed onto the hatches of the nose equipment bays.
• Extensive fire protection was provided by means of heat insulation screens housed in the tail, engine nacelles and internal bays adjacent to the fuel tanks (applied on 10th Series aircraft only), as well as a two-stage fire extinguishing system inside engine bays.
• The collector tank was protected by 8mm steel plating on the bottom and rear walls, while the side walls were made with 18mm aluminium alloy plating.
• The flat bulletproof windshield was 70mm thick, made capable of withstanding hits from 12.7mm projectiles.
• The ejection seat was supplied with an armoured headrest for the pilot, providing protection from bullets and high-speed missile warhead fragments coming from above and the rear.

The Frogfoot driver enjoys a particularly good side protection as he sits deep in a titanium armour bath and also has armour plating above his ejection seat. (Author)

resistance to small-arms fire and high-speed missile warhead fragments. The combat survivability features, as incorporated in the design of the basic Su-25s built before mid-1987, accounted for some 7.5 per cent of the aircraft's normal take-off weight (1,320lb [600kg]), while the machines built after mid-1987 introduced vastly improved self-protection features for the airframe and engines, accounting for 11.5 per cent of the aircraft's normal take-off weight, which translated into 2,420lb (1,100kg).

Navigation, attack and communication equipment

The KN-23-1 analogue navigation system included the IKV-1 inertial reference and heading gyro system, the RSBN-6S short-range (tactical) aid to navigation/instrument landing system, the ARK-15M automatic direction finder, the DISS-7 Doppler navigation system, the SVS-1-72-1VS air data system, the A-01 Reper-M radar altimeter, the MRP-56P marker beacon receiver and the Pyon antenna-feeder system.

The communication equipment included one R-862 Zhuravl'-30 UHF/VHF radio set used for air-to-air and air-to-ground communication, while the R-828 Evkalypt UHF radio set was used for communication with the land forces on the battlefield or between the aircraft when operating in formation.

The Su-25 was equipped with the SRO-1P (SRO-2M on the first production machines) IFF transponder and the SO-69 ATC transponder.

The basic Su-25 featured an all-analogue attack suite, designated the SUO-T8-54. It included the Klyon-PS laser rangefinder/target designator – seeing through a small window in the nose – and an ASP-17BTs-8 electro-optical weapons sight for aiming the cannon and rockets and dropping bombs against visually distinguishable ground and air targets.

The aircraft was also equipped with the Tester-U3 crash-resistant flight data recorder, as well as the SSh-45-1-100OS camera gun looking through the weapons sight, the AKS-5-75-OS forward-looking camera in the nose and the MS-61 Lyra tape audio recorder.

The most powerful guided weapon that the classic Su-25 can deploy is the Kh-29L (AS-14 Kedge) laser-guided missile, weighing some 1,498lb (700kg). It is used mainly for destroying hardened bunkers and other small-size/high-value targets on the battlefield. (Krasimir Grozev)

Ordnance

The Su-25's ordnance was carried on ten underwing hardpoints. The four inboard hardpoints under each wing were provided with either BD-3-25 pylons or MBD-2-67U multiple bomb carrier beams (also known as multiple ejector racks), on which all the types of bombs, rockets and gun pods – cleared for the type – could be suspended. The outboard hardpoint under each wing was provided with a PD-62-8 pylon to install the APU-60-1MD launch rail for the R-60 or R-60M air-to-air missile.

The Su-25s (both single- and two-seaters) built for the Soviet Air Force were also made capable of deploying one RN-28 adjustable-yield nuclear bomb.

The list of the guided missiles in the Su-25's arsenal included the R-60 or R-60M air-to-air missile and the Kh-25ML (up to four), the S-25L (up to four) and the Kh-29L (up to two) laser-guided air-to-surface missiles. The unguided weapons selection included the S-5 57mm and S-8 80mm rockets;

B **Su-25 MUNITIONS**

Guided missiles
1. Kh-29L (AS-14 Kedge) laser-guided air-to-surface missile
2. Kh-25ML (AS-10 Karen) laser-guided air-to-surface missile
3. Kh-58U (AS-11 Kilter) anti-radar missile
4. R-60 (AA-8 Aphid) air-to-air missile
5. R-73 (AA-11 Archer) air-to-air missile
Rockets
6. S-24 240mm rocket
7. S-25OFM 250mm rocket in launch tube and in flight
8. S-8 80mm rocket fired from the B8M1 20-round rocket pack
9. S-13 122mm missile (fired from the B13 five-round rocket pack)
Bombs
10. FAB-500ShN 500kg parachute-retarded bomb
11. OFAB-250-270 250kg free-fall bomb
Guns
12. VPU-17A cannon pack
13. SPPU-22-01 pod fitted with a depressable 23mm cannon

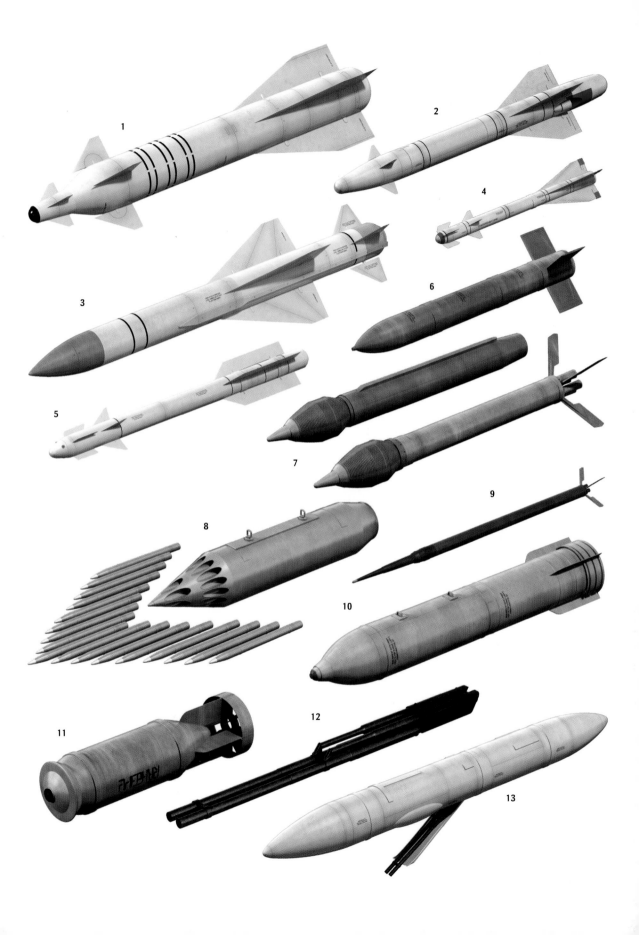

The GSh-30 30mm twin-barrel gun, integrated into the Su-25 in the form of the VPU-17A gun pack – seen here equipped with the late-style single-piece muzzle – was provided with 300 rounds and sported a rate of fire of 3,000rpm. (Author)

the former fired from 16- and 32-round pods (UB-16 and UB-32 respectively) and the latter from 20-round pods (B8M). The Su-25 was also cleared to fire two types of large-calibre rockets, the S-24 (240mm) and S-25 (250mm), with up to four being carried on single launch rails. It was also made capable of deploying up to four SPPU-22-01 gun pods with GSh-23 twin-barrelled cannon, flexibly mounted (the maximum downwards deflection angle was 30°), installed forward- or aft-facing and provided with 250 rounds, or the SPPU-687 with flexibly mounted GSh-301 30mm cannon (the maximum downwards deflection angle was 30° in vertical plane and 15° left and right in the horizontal plane).

Kh-29L (AS-14 Kedge) laser-guided missile

The Kh-29L was a tactical air-to-ground missile used for destruction of small-size hardened targets, such as steel-reinforced concrete shelters of various types, concrete runways, large rail and road bridges and small- to medium-class ships.

The missile had a 755lb (317kg) shaped-charge warhead with contact and delayed fuse. The Su-25 was cleared to carry up to two missiles under the innermost pylons on the AKU-58 ejector racks, launched from low and medium level in shallow dive. Useful launch range was between 1.1 and 5.4nm (2 and 10km), while the missile demonstrated Circular Error Probable (CEP) within 13ft (4m) when lasing the target with the launch aircraft's own Klyon-PS laser designator system.

R-60 air-to-air missile

The supersonic and lightweight air-to-air missile was mainly intended for self-defence and used an infra-red (heat-seeking homing) guidance system.

The minimum launch range (a significant parameter in the dogfight) of the R-60 and its improved derivative, designated the R-60M, was only 960ft (300m) and the probability of hit with a twin-missile salvo was quoted as 0.7–0.8.

S-24 rocket

The 240mm rocket, a powerful yet precise unguided weapon for destroying hardened small-size targets, was fired from a single-round rail APU-7D or APU-68 launcher. It weighed 517lb (235kg) and had a warhead weighing 270lb (123 kg). The maximum speed was 1,356ft/s (413m/s), while range was up to 6,648ft (2,000m) and the lethal radius of the warhead was between 1,000 and 1,313ft (300 and 400m).

When used for area suppression purposes, the S-24 was equipped with a proximity fuse set to detonate it at 100ft (33m) altitude above terrain for an improved destructive effect of the fragments, covering a large ellipse-shaped area.

VPU-17A gun pack	One GSh-30 (AO-17B) 30mm twin-barrel cannon, built into the port side of the forward fuselage, under the pilot's cockpit. Muzzle port was situated just behind the nosecone, offset to port. The gun fired a range of highly destructive 13oz (390g) projectiles
Weight	231lb (105kg)
Rate of fire	3,000rpm
Muzzle velocity	2,853ft/s (870m/s)
Effective firing range	2,620 and 4,921ft (800 and 1,500m)
Magazine capacity	250 rounds
Barrel life	4,000 rounds; maximum burst length was five seconds and 250 rounds

A Frogfoot pictured here behind an impressive array of guided and unguided weapons, including the ZAB-500 napalm canisters displayed in the centre, FAN-500ShN retarded bombs, ODAB-500P thermobaric bombs, BETAB-500 concrete-penetrating bombs and FAB-500M-62 high-explosive bombs on the sides. (Krasimir Grozev)

Klyon-PS laser rangefinder-designator

The nose-mounted Klyon-PS system measured slant range to the target selected by the pilot with 16ft (5m) accuracy, which was useful for rocket and bomb deployment, providing laser designation of targets for firing the Kh-25L, Kh-29L and S-25L laser-guided missiles.

The maximum measured slant range was 2.7nm (5km) and the laser beam was manually steered by the pilot 12° left and right, 6° up and 30° down. The system's effective range was between 1,320 and 16,500ft (400 and 5,000m).

Su-25 dimensions

Variant	Wingspan	Length, overall	Height	Wing area, gross	Tailplane span
Su-25	47ft 1in (14.36m)	50ft 4in (15.53m)	15ft 9in (4.80m)	362.75sq ft (33.7m²)	15ft 3in (4.65m)
Su-25UB	47ft 1in (14.36m)	50ft 4in (15.53m)	17ft 0in (5.20m)	362.75sq ft (33.7m²)	15ft 3in (4.65m)
Su-25T	47ft 1in (14.36m)	50ft 4in (15.35m)	17ft 0in (5.20m)	324sq ft (30.10m²)	(15ft 0in) 4.58m

Su-25 weight

Variant	Empty	Normal	Max take-off	Max landing	Take-off run
Su-25 (10th Series Production Standard)	20,950lb (9,500kg)	32,024lb (14,530kg)	38,636bs (17,530kg)	29,320lb (13,300kg)	1,970ft (600m)
Su-25UB	22,568lb (10,240kg)	33,712lb (15,300kg)	45,121lb (18,500kg)	29,320lb (13,300kg)	1,970ft (600m)
Su-25T	23,516lb (10,670)	36,542bs (16,580kg)	42,978bs (19,500kg)	29,100lb (13,200kg)	2,135ft (650m)
Su-25TM	24,487lb (10,740 kg)	37,445bs (16,990kg)	45,182bs (20,500kg)	29,100lb (13,200kg)	2,135ft (650m)

Su-25 performance

Variant	Max speed sea level	Max attack speed	Combat ceiling	Combat radius	Ferry range
Su-25*	512kt (950km/h)	372kt (690km/h)	22,960ft (7,000m)	148nm (275km)	1,012nm (1,980km)
Su-25UB	512kt (950km/h)	372kt (690km/h)	22,960ft (7,000m)	248nm (400km)	1,081nm (2000km)
Su-25T/TM**	512kt (950km/h)	372kt (690km/h)	32,800ft (10,000m)	248nm (400km)	1,214nm (2,250km)

* The speed at sea level, the combat ceiling and the combat radius at low level were recorded with 2 tonnes of bombs (four FAB-500M-62 bombs) and two R-60 air-to-air missiles

** The Su-25T/TM, the combat radius was recorded at low level

Su-25 main production (1978–91)

Variant	Number built	First flight
Su-25	582	June 1979
Su-25K	180	1984
Su-25BM	50	March 1990
Su-25UB	approx. 100	August 1985
Su-25UBK	28	1986
Su-25UTG	13	September 1988
Su-25T	12	July 1985

Su-25 VERSIONS, MODIFICATIONS AND PROJECTS

Su-25K for export customers

The Su-25K (internal design bureau designation T8K) was the export derivative of the Frogfoot, developed in 1984 in two versions. The A-version was delivered only to Warsaw Pact member states, such as Czechoslovakia and Bulgaria, while the B-version was sold to other customers from the Third World – Iraq, Angola and North Korea.

The A-version was almost identical to the VVS baseline version and the list of differences included only the IFF (the SRO-2 instead of SRO-1P) and encryption equipment; it was also stripped from the equipment, enabling it to deliver nuclear weapons. The B-version of the Su-25K, however, had some restricted weapons options, with no capabilities to employ air-to-ground guided missiles. As many as 180 Su-25Ks were manufactured in Tbilisi between 1984 and 1989. A small number of these export Frogfoots built in the late 1980s remained in the Soviet Union and then in Russia – the Su-25Ks were originally intended to be used for conversion training of foreign pilots from the customer nations at the Kushtevskaya airfield, belonging to the Krasnodar Higher Pilot Training School. In the 1990s, these export-grade Frogfoots were assigned to a front-line unit, the 461st ShAP stationed at Krasnodar, which saw participation in both war campaigns in Chechnya and then in the war campaign in South Ossetia.

Two-seater Frogfoots

The Su-25K was the export derivative of the first-generation jet Shturmovik, featuring a few differences to the standard Soviet Frogfoot-A, with an old-style IFF and lacking the wiring and control panels to employ the RN-28 nuclear bomb. (Author)

The two-seat derivative of the Su-25, featuring heavily stepped cockpits, was conceived for the first time in 1976 and, one year later, the design, wearing the internal designation T8-UB, was approved. The first five fuselages were assembled at Aviation Plant No. 99 in Ulan-Ude – now known as Ulan-Ude Aviation Plant (U-UAP) – in 1984, though three were subsequently handed over to Aviation Plant No. 31 in Tbilisi for conversion to the T-8M standard. In order to compensate for the development delay, it was decided to shorten the two-seater's factory flight test programme, aiming to complete it by the end of 1985.

The first Su-25 two-seater, designated the T8-UB1, was completed in June 1985 and undertook its maiden flight in Ulan-Ude on 10 August, in the hands of Sukhoi test pilot A. Ivanov. It was then transported by air in disassembled state to the Sukhoi flight test station at Zhukovskii and, after installing additional flight data recording equipment, the T8-UB1 was re-flown on 10 October 1985. Its shortened factory flight testing phase was completed by 13 December the same year.

The second two-seater, designated the T8-UB2, was flown for the first time in Ulan-Ude on 14 November 1985. In 1986, both the T8-UBs were handed over to the VVS for participation in the Su-25UB's state testing effort, including combat employment trials, which was completed by March 1987. The series production was launched in 1986 and the first two-seaters, receiving the service designation Su-25UB, were handed over to both the VVS and three export customers in 1987. The export two-seater derivative of the Frogfoot received the designation Su-25UBK (internal design bureau designation T8-UBK).

The two-seater Frogfoot was developed following the minimum changes concept, with the second (instructor's) cockpit inserted into the place of the fuselage fuel tank under a common canopy, with separate sideways-opening sections, dual controls, improved electrical and hydraulic systems, as well as a new life-support system with increased-capacity oxygen storage. The rear cockpit was raised by 1.44ft (0.44m), providing the instructor pilot with a 7° view over the nose, while the front cockpit's viewing angle was retained the same as that of the single-seater – 19° over the nose. In order to improve the instructor pilot's view further, the rear canopy was provided with a retractable periscope and its cockpit received a dedicated panel for simulation of various malfunctions of essential flight and navigation instruments during proficiency check rides. The two-seater Frogfoot retained the full targeting suite of its single-seat counterpart and was capable of deploying all unguided and guided weapons cleared for the Su-25.

The second cockpit necessitated a slight reduction in the fuselage fuel tank capacity, by about 550lb (250kg), while the armoured

The Su-25UB/UBK two-seater had its second cockpit inserted in place of the fuselage fuel tank, under a common canopy provided with separate sideways-opening sections, and the instructor was provided with a good forward view. (Author)

The two-seater prototype of the Frogfoot was flown for the first time in September 1985 and, in the following year, the Su-25UB/UBK was launched in production at the aviation plant in Ulan-Ude for both the VVS and the three existing export customers at the time. (Andrey Zinchuk)

An Su-25UTG hooked trainer assigned to the 279th OKIAP – the sole Russian Naval Aviation fast-jet unit – is captured by the camera here taking off from the ski jump of the NITKA carrier desk simulation centre in Saki in Crimea, Ukraine, during a training deployment in September 2009. (Andrey Zinchuk)

bathtub of welded titanium plates for the front cockpit was retained the same as that of the single-seater. The pilot in the second cockpit was protected in the front by the rear side of the bath and from the rear by an armoured plate, while the intakes provided partial side-on protection. A pair of initial-production Su-25UBs, earmarked for service with the 378th OShAP in Afghanistan, received reinforced rear cockpit protection in the form of scabbed-on steel armour plates.

The Su-25UB's pronounced hump, caused by the insertion of the instructor's cockpit, necessitated some clever design alterations in order to retain the stability performance as close as possible to that of the single-seater. This was achieved by introducing an increased-area tailfin; simply by adding a 400mm plug into the base and altering its profile.

The Su-25UB's fuel system was also redesigned and improved, with two fuselage tanks, one centre-wing section tank and two wing tanks, for a total fuel volume of 3,685l. The two-seater, in contrast to its single-seater counterpart, introduced a centralized refuelling system for receiving fuel under pressure, resulting in a much shorter refuelling time. All the fuselage and centre-wing tanks were composed of rubber bag-type sections with double-layer rubber protection and were filled with reticulated foam.

The Su-25UT was an unarmed two-seater derivative developed in 1987. It lacked the Su-25UB's weapons systems and armour protection and was intended for use as a dedicated jet trainer, replacing both the Aero L-29 and L-39 jets, operated by the DOSAAF paramilitary flight training organization. Lightened by some 4,400lb (2,000kg), it boasted much better manoeuvrability than its combat-capable brethren. The Su-25UT prototype was produced by conversion of the T8-UB1 aircraft and received the new designations T8-UT-1; later on, it received the new in-service designation Su-28. In the event, it remained in prototype form only, as the Su-28 proved to be quite expensive for use as a jet trainer, while for use as a high-performance aerobatic machine it was deemed too heavy and underpowered.

C

1. Chad is among the latest customers of the Frogfoot, receiving from Ukraine two single-seaters and one two-seater in 2008.
2. In 2009 Equatorial Guinea purchased from Ukraine two Su-25UB two-seaters, reportedly upgraded to the Su-25UBM1 standard.
3. A Su-25U in Georgian Air Force colours. This is the latest two-seater derivative of the Frogfoot, built by Tbilisi Aircraft Manufacturing in the early 2000s, using surplus Su-25T fuselages mated to new cockpit sections, supplied by U-UAP. At least seven such two-seaters, powered by the uprated R-195 turbojet, are believed to have been built, two of which were delivered to the Georgian air arm.
4. This Frogfoot-A is among the ten ex-Slovak Su-25Ks and one Su-25UBK purchased in 2004 by Armenia. This particular aircraft, wearing serial '18', is a former Slovak Air Force '1006'.

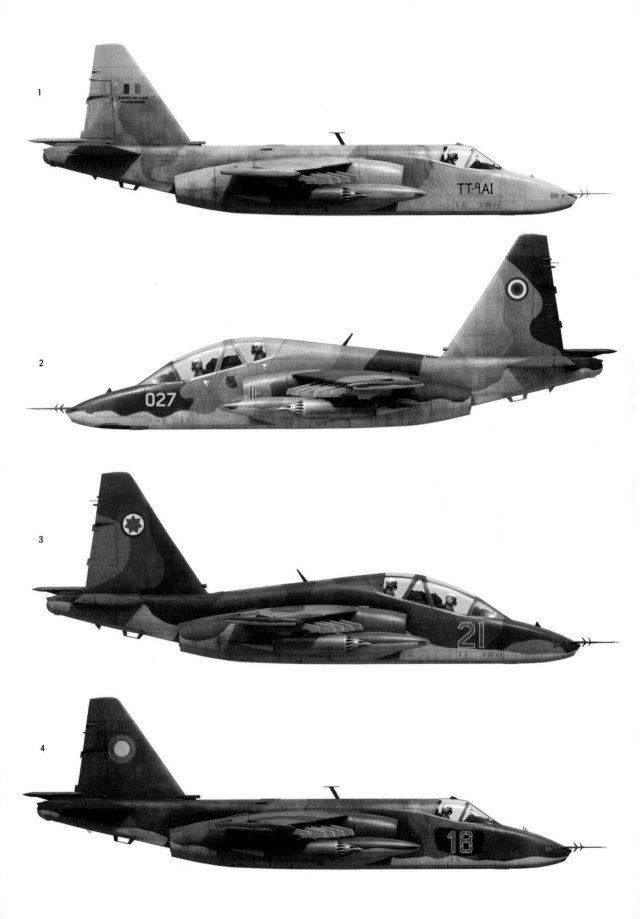

1

2

3

4

Su-25UTG for carrier landing training

The design experience accumulated during the work on the Su-25UT was later utilized during the development of the Su-25UTG navalized carrier-borne hook-equipped trainer for the Soviet Navy's aviation service. After a successful series of ski-jump trials involving the T8-4 single-seat prototype, it was decided to continue with the development of the Su-25UTG navalized two-seater and, in the course of this programme, a production-standard Su-25UB (factory number 05–10) was converted at Ulan-Ude in early 1988 to act as the UTG prototype. During this conversion, the fuselage structure was reinforced and the entire targeting suite and weapons systems were deleted, as well as part of the underwing pylons (only four pylons were retained for drop tanks) and the engine armour protection.

The Su-25UTG received a retractable arrester hook, attached to a reinforced rear fuselage load-carrying structural beam, while the shortened rear fuselage lacked the brake parachute housing. The tailplane was also redesigned, and the aircraft received the A-380 carrier-borne tactical aid to navigation and instrument landing system. Due to the design complexity, it was eventually decided that wing folding was not required, in order to reduce costs and shorten development time.

The Su-25UTG prototype – designated the T8-UTG1 – was flown for the first time in Ulan-Ude on 1 September 1988 and, on 24 October the same year, it was ferried to the naval aviation test base in Saki on the Crimea Peninsula (now in Ukraine) for trials on the NITKA (officially known under the abbreviation NIUTK) deck simulation complex, equipped with a ski jump and an arrester wire system. The first landing using the arrester hook at the NITKA site was made on 13 December 1988.

The Su-25UTG prototype, in the hands of Sukhoi test pilot Igor Votintsev, performed its first deck landing on the then-Soviet *Tbilisi* (now renamed as *Admiral Kuznetsov*), a heavy aircraft-carrying cruiser, on 1 November 1989 and reported its first deck take-off the next day.

The flight testing and evaluation programme was carried out between September 1988 and February 1990 and, based on its positive outcome, the Su-25UTG was eventually recommended for introduction into service for training deck pilots, who planned then to convert to the Su-27K and MiG-29K fighters. The deck-specific training on the Su-25UTG was to be performed mainly using the NITKA simulation facility. The carrier trials of the Su-25UTG took place in September and October 1991, including a series of 25 landings and take-offs, with a take-off run of 643ft (195m).

A production batch of ten Su-25UTGs rolled off the line at U-UAP in 1990, followed by three further examples later in the decade; the survivors are still in operation with the Russian Naval Aviation's 297th OKIAP (Ship-Based Fighter Air Regiment), stationed at Severomorsk-3 airfield near the northern city of Murmansk. In mid-2012, the regiment had seven aircraft and between three and four of them were maintained in airworthy condition.

After the dissolution of the Soviet Union in 1991, two of the first production Su-25UTGs, used for trials in Saki, were retained by the newly established armed forces of Ukraine. In 2007, one of these was sold out to China, while the other was handed over to Russia in exchange for an Su-25UB.

Never-built versions

In 1991, the Sukhoi Design Bureau worked on a design for a three-seat trainer project, designated the Su-25U3 and named Russkaya Troyka (Russian Trio). Provided with seating for one instructor and two trainees, it featured three separate cockpits accommodated in a tandem scheme. No prototypes were built, however, and the project was eventually abandoned in 1993.

There was another carrier-capable derivative of the Frogfoot, the single-seat Su-25K (T8-K), which was originally conceived in 1976 as a true carrier-borne attack aircraft, optimized for operations against small ships and coastal defence installations, as well as for suppression of ship air defences and use against airborne early-warning aircraft. It was to be equipped with an all-weather nav/attack system and telescopic nose undercarriage with mechanism for launch catapult attachment, folding wings and in-flight refuelling equipment, while its weapons suite was to include laser- and TV-guided missiles. In the event, there were no in-depth design works on this very sophisticated carrier derivative of the Frogfoot and it remained a paper project only. The list of the paper projects also includes the Su-25R, a dedicated tactical reconnaissance aircraft, as well as the Su-25B, a single-seater utilizing the Su-25UB fuselage and featuring increased-volume fuel tanks, R-195 engines and improved mission equipment.

Su-25T Super Frogfoot

First design work on the T8M project (later designated the Su-25T) began in 1976. This enhanced Frogfoot derivative was designed in accordance with the concept, calling for a sophisticated platform with advanced targeting equipment and firing relatively simple and affordable guided missiles. This was in stark contrast to the original Fairchild A-10 Thunderbolt design concept, which called for an unsophisticated well-protected platform capable of firing advanced guided missiles against armoured small-size targets on the battlefield.

The T8M was required to boast far better combat effectiveness and survivability than the 'vanilla' Su-25, thanks to the extensive use of guided stand-off weapons and more advanced targeting sensors combined with a highly automated integrated flight/navigation suite. In order to satisfy the requirements, it received a plethora of enhanced combat survivability features, such as extensive polyurethane foam fuel tank filling and protective coatings, as well as fuel lines and control runs being better protected from combat damage, while the fuel system and avionics compartment had to be provided with more effective fire protection. In the event, the total weight of the T8M's airframe combat survivability features reached an impressive 2,453lb (1,115kg).

This radically redesigned Frogfoot single-seater utilized the Su-25UB's humped airframe, with the rear cockpit faired over and internal space used to house many new avionics boxes and an extra tonne of fuel to double the range compared with the standard Su-25. The T8M's total fuel capacity reached 8,448lb

The Su-25T was a highly automated Frogfoot derivative, capable of using a wide array of guided weapons but, in the event, it failed to enter into full-scale production and the last examples in regular service are known to have operated with the RuAF's combat training centre at Lipetsk until the late 2000s. (Andrey Zinchuk)

(3,840kg) and, in a bid to provide additional internal volume, the cannon and ammunition bay were deleted. The GSh-30 cannon was scabbed on below the fuselage, offset to starboard by 10.5in (270mm), and the externally mounted gun pack received the new designation NPPU-8M. The T8M also received hydraulic actuators for the elevator controls.

The new derivative featured an entirely new targeting system installed in an enlarged nosecone. The I-251M Shkval nav/attack system integrated a TV system, a Prichal laser rangefinder/target designator and a Vikhr ATGM laser-beam missile homing system. The high-resolution TV system had a wide Field of View (FoV) mode, covering 36° x 27° picture and usable for target search, while the narrow FoV (1° x 0.7°) was used for target tracking, providing 25x scene zoom. The system's Line of Sight (LoS) was capable of steering through 70° in azimuth (i.e. on the horizontal plane) and from 15° above the centreline and 80° below (i.e. on the vertical plane). The system was advertized as capable of tracking moving tank-size targets and designating them for missile launch at ranges of up to 4.3nm (8km), with the laser designator illuminating a 16.6ft x 16.4ft (5m x 5m) box. The system was also advertized as being capable of detecting a bridge from 11 to 13nm (20 to 24km), and single buildings were detected from 8.1nm (15km). When used against air targets, the Shkval was capable of detecting fighter aircraft from 5.4nm (10km) and helicopters from 3.2nm (6km).

The 9A4172 Vikhr missile came equipped with a tandem warhead said to be capable of penetrating between 800 and 1,000mm of armour after dealing with dynamic protection (i.e. reactive armour). During the tests, a Vikhr scored a direct hit in a tank turret from a distance of 5.4nm (10km). A total of 16 Vikhr missiles with armour penetration capability of up to 900mm were carried on two eight-round underwing launchers, in addition to all 1980s-vintage Soviet-made laser- and TV-guided missiles and bombs.

A pod-installed Khod FLIR equipment was tested on the Su-25T, as well as the podded Merkuriy low-light level TV system, but both systems reported little success due to the unimpressive state of Soviet, and then Russian, developments in the defence electronics area, eventually failing to demonstrate adequate range and reliability performance.

The navigation system was made by the A-723 long-range and A-312-10 short-range aids to navigation, as well as the IK-VK-80-4 reference gyro platform and the ARK-22 ADF. It made possible flights to and from combat areas under largely automatic control, thanks to the sophisticated autopilot system. While approaching the targets, the Shkval system was activated automatically at 5.4nm (10km) from the target and was then steered to detect it and perform tracking with an accuracy of 2ft (0.6m) to enable a Vikhr ATGM launch.

The sophisticated Irtish self-protection suite comprised an L150 Pastel-K RWR (also used to cue the seekers of the Kh-25MP and Kh-31P anti-radar missiles), the L166S1 Sukhogruz IR lamp-based jammer, UV-26 chaff-flare dispensers with a total of 192 rounds and the L-203I Gardenya-1FU pod-mounted radar jammer.

The first Su-25T prototype – known as the T8M-1 – was flown for the first time on 17 August 1984 in the hands of Sukhoi test pilot A. Isakov. It was soon followed by two more prototypes and eight Tbilisi-built pre-production aircraft, which were intended to be used in the flight test programme, while another airframe was destined for use for ground static testing. The flight and design testing effort was completed by June 1987, taking about 500 sorties, but, due to the low reliability demonstrated by the Su-25T, it entered the next testing phase – the so-called state testing effort – during 1988. The first portion of this far more

This Su-25TM, serialled 82, was upgraded in 1995 from an Su-25T at U-UAP, to be used by Sukhoi and the RuAF's Flight Test Centre at Akhtubinsk for evaluation and testing purposes. (U-UAZ)

comprehensive testing and evaluation phase (the so-called stage A) was performed at the Soviet Air Force Flight Test Centre at Akhtubinsk and completed by 1990.

Completion of Stage A allowed the aircraft to be launched in low-rate production in the Tbilisi plant and the two aircraft for participation in the state testing effort – designated as the T8M-4 and T8M-5 – were rolled out in 1989, using re-worked Su-25UB airframes supplied from Ulan-Ude. Stage B was completed in September 1993, and the Su-25T was eventually recommended for introduction in service with the then Russian Air Force. A total of eight aircraft, including the three prototypes, one of which (the T8M-2) was lost in June 1991, were involved in the flight test programme that saw over 3,000 flights and no less than 40 Vikhr live launches.

The first machine of the 12-aircraft operational trials batch to be built in Tbilisi was flight-tested for the first time in June 1990, but only six pre-production Su-25Ts are know to have been taken on strength by the VVS, operated by the Lipetsk-based 4th Combat Training and Aircrew Conversion Centre. The new type received its baptism of fire during the second Chechen war in 1999, logging some 20 combat sorties.

The promising attack aircraft – featuring rather sophisticated weaponry and sensors – had the bad luck to approach the completion of its extensive flight test programme at the wrong time, as the Soviet Union and its mighty aviation industry and air force suddenly collapsed in 1991. Some analysts still argue that there was no urgent need in the 1990s for such highly specialized, quite expensive and somewhat over-sophisticated new anti-tank aircraft to enter service with the violently downsized and poorly financed RuAF.

Not surprisingly, in the early and mid-1990s, in the wake of the dissolution of the Soviet Union, the Su-25T's programme reported disappointingly slow progress. Some 17 fully or partially completed Su-25T airframes from the initial batches were left in the Tbilisi plant, along with about three dozen basic Su-25s in various states of assembly. A number of these uncompleted Su-25Ts were converted during the 2000s into the Su-25U two-seater version, using new cockpit sections supplied by U-UAP. At least seven such two-seaters, powered by the uprated R-195 turbojet, were built and two of these were delivered to the Georgian Air Force, while the rest are said to have been exported to Azerbaijan and Turkmenistan.

All-weather Su-25TM

The night-capable, all-weather and further upgraded Su-25T derivative, designated the Su-25TM (design bureau designation T8TM), was conceived in 1986. This variant was to feature a sophisticated targeting suite, including the pod-mounted Kinzhal millimetric radar and/or the Khod FLIR systems. However, radar and FLIR trials in the early 1990s revealed that both the systems had lower-than-expected performance and reliability. That is why the Phazotron-NIIR Kopyo 3cm radar was chosen in the early 1990s as the main targeting sensor for use in adverse-weather and low-altitude operations. New mission equipment also included the two-pod MSP-410 Omul EW system, and the Su-25TM was able to use a wide variety of new precision-guided air-to-surface and air-to-air weapons, such as the Kh-35U and Kh-31A anti-ship missiles and the R-27R/ER and R-77 air-to-air missiles.

Two of the existing Su-25Ts were upgraded in the early 1990s to be used as Su-25TM development platforms. These were the T8M-1, redesignated the T8TM-1, and the T8M-4, redesignated the T8TM-2. The former made its maiden flight in its new guise on 4 February 1991, and served as the testing and evaluation platform of the Khod FLIR and the new EW system. The T-8TM-2 was used in the trials of the Kinzhal radar, and later for the enhanced Shkval-M electro-optical targeting system development, as well as for the further improved SUO-39P weapons control system. In late 1994, the T8TM-2 was fitted with a dummy Kopyo-25 radar pod on the centreline hardpoint and, in August 1995, this aircraft was displayed at the MAKS-1995 exhibition. The Phazotron Kopyo-25 centimetric radar – with maximum detection range against main battle tanks quoted as 13nm (25km) – was intended to replace the Kinzhal, which demonstrated disappointingly low reliability.

The first newly built Super Frogfoot (T8TM-3) to be assembled at U-UAP, wearing the serial '20', took to the air on 15 August 1995, followed by the second (T8TM-4) on 15 March 1998, as it was intended to replace the T-8TM-1, which had run out of service life by that time.

The former was used in the aerodynamic trials with the Kopyo-25's pod, whereas the latter featured the full-standard SUO-39P fire control system, including the Kopyo-25 radar and a complete self-protection suite comprising the SIO-1 RWR and the MSP-410 pod-mounted radar jammer. The Kopyo-25 trials on the Su-25TM commenced in February 1999.

By mid-2002, the Su-25TM prototypes logged some 120 test sorties in the course of the type's prolonged state testing and evaluation effort, the completion of which was estimated to take no fewer than 600 sorties.

Despite its vastly increased overall combat capability, the Su-25TM ultimately failed to attract any significant funding support from the Russian ministry of defence in the late 1990s/early 2000s and, as a consequence, the improved Super Frogfoot was dropped from the RuAF's priorities.

The over-sophisticated Su-25TM was proposed as an attack aircraft with a wide array of guided weapons for all-weather operations. Here, the second production example with underfuselage Kopyo pod is seen carrying a rather eclectic weapons mix, including the Kh-58U ARM, Kh-29T ASM, a cluster of Vikhr ATGMs, as well as the R-77 and R-73 AAMs. (Sukhoi Shturmoviks Company)

Su-25SM – the RuAF's current upgrade standard

The need to extend the Su-25's service life and enhance the mission avionics capability of the RuAF's existing front-line fleet started to be addressed seriously in 1998, when it finally became clear that the over-sophisticated, untried and rather expensive Su-25TM would not enter squadron service in the near future. Initially, the Sukhoi Shturmoviks company proposed that the basic Frogfoot fleet in Russia should be extensively upgraded through the introduction of a sophisticated integrated digital nav/attack suite, with most components borrowed from the Su-25TM, including a nose-mounted Kopyo-25 radar set.

The upgraded Su-25SMs of the Budyonnovsk-based RuAF attack regiment (368th OShAP) saw their baptism of fire in the bloody five-day battle with Georgia in August 2008. (Andrey Zinchuk)

However, the eventual upgrade standard approved by the RuAF in 2000 proved to be considerably downscaled when compared to the initial plans, as the service decided to keep its Su-25s flying for two decades to come and, investing in some modest avionics enhancements combined with airframe refurbishment, to extend the Frogfoot's service life to 2,500 hours, with an option for a further extension to 4,000 hours.

The Su-25SM (Stroyevoy, Modernizirovannyi – Line Upgrade) in its original guise was conceived in the early 2000s and regarded as a relatively low-cost approach to bring the analogue Frogfoot into the modern digital age. Its all-new PRnK-25SM Bars nav/attack suite was built around the BTsVM-90 digital computer, borrowed from the Su-25TM. Most of the analogue components of the original KN-23-1 nav/attack suite – suffering from poor reliability and considered maintenance intensive – were replaced by new digital equipment. Navigation preciseness provided by the new PrNK-25SM suite was said to be within 46ft (15m) using satellite correction and 660ft (200m) without; this great improvement became possible thanks to the integration of the A-737-01 GPS/GLONASS satellite navigation receiver, providing navigation accuracy of some 0.2 per cent deviation from track on a typical route. The high positioning preciseness in turn facilitated precise navigation (i.e. non-visual) bombing runs in poor weather and, at night, against fixed targets with known positions using unguided bombs.

A new head-up display (HUD), the KAI-1-01, providing two times greater FoV than that of the simple ASP-17BTs-8 electro-optical sight, was also added. Other components added during the upgrade included a multi-function cockpit display (used to display a digital map and flight, navigation and tactical information), an RSBN-85 short-range aid to navigation, an ARK-35-1 automatic direction finder, a Karat-B-25 flight data recorder, a Berkut-1 video recording system, a Banker-2 UHF/VHF comms radio, an SO-96 transponder and an L150 Pastel radar warning receiver. The Su-25SM's R-95Sh engine received an anti-surge system to improve resistance to ingestion of powder gases while firing the gun and rockets in salvoes.

The combination of the new HUD, weapons computer and nav/attack system's digital components promised significantly increased preciseness when employing unguided ordnance, with improvement advertised as being between two and three times greater. It was notable that no new TV-guided precision-guided munitions were conceived for addition to the Su-25SM's

The Russian air arm will maintain a fleet of 130 upgraded Su-25SMs – this quantity was deemed enough for equipping no fewer than nine front-line squadrons, plus one or two training squadrons. (Andrey Zinchuk)

weapons suite in its original guise, but its air-to-air capability was expanded with the R-73 highly agile missile, albeit without a helmet-mounted cueing.

The newly added ground attack weapons included the S-13T 130mm rockets (carried in five-round B-13 pods) with blast-fragmentation and armour-piercing warheads; in addition, the Su-25SM was made capable of launching the existing Kh-25ML and Kh-29L laser-guided missiles while in horizontal flight and firing two missiles at two different targets in a single firing pass. The GSh-30-2 cannon with 250 rounds received three new reduced rate-of-fire modes – in order to increase the number of firing passes – allowing for 20, 40 and 80 seconds of total firing time respectively.

The Su-25SM also received the new BD3-25 underwing pylons. The overall weight savings thanks to the use of new, lighter equipment and avionics accounted for some 660lb (300kg).

The upgrade programme, however, suffered from considerable delays from the very beginning. Eventually, the first Su-25SM prototype, wearing at the time the serial '33', took the air on 5 March 2002 in the hands of Sukhoi test pilot Igor Solovyov, and the test and evaluation programme was completed in 2006.

The first batch of six production-upgraded Su-25SMs were officially handed over to the RuAF on 28 December 2006, with six further upgrades following suit in 2007 and another eight in 2008. In 2009, 12 Su-25SMs were rolled out, 12 in 2010 and eight in 2011, while in 2012 another batch of 12 upgraded Frogfoots was reported to have been funded by the Russian ministry of defence.

The first six production-upgraded Frogfoots were delivered initially to the RuAF's Lipetsk-based combat training and aircrew conversion centre and then, in 2007, deliveries switched to one of the squadrons of the 368th ShAP, stationed in Budyonnovsk. This Frogfoot unit has been known since 2010 as an aviation group, assigned to the 6972nd air base, headquartered at Krymsk, and has three Su-25 squadrons, two of which are equipped with upgraded aircraft; the first Su-25UBM upgraded two-seater was expected in the end of 2012. By mid-2012, the second Su-25-equipped group of the 6972nd air base, stationed at Primorsko-Akhtarsk and operating two Frogfoot squadrons, began to receive its first Su-25SMs. In 2011–12, the two squadrons of the attack aviation group stationed at Tchernigovka airfield and assigned to 6988th air base (headquartered at Khurba) also converted to the upgraded Frogfoot.

D | **RUSSIAN AIR FORCE Su-25 OF THE SOUTH OSSETIAN WAR**

This Su-25 belongs to the 461st ShAP (Attack Aviation Regiment), a prominent combat unit, at the time stationed at Krasnodar in the south part of Russia and subordinated to the 1st Attack Division of the Russian Air Force's 4th Air Army. The unit was involved in the second day of the war in South Ossetia, 9 August 2008, and flew a number of highly effective CAS missions, pounding the Georgian forces positioned around the South Ossetian capital, Tskhinvali. The aircraft of the two squadrons of the regiment wore the 'chained dog' badge on both sides of the nose, the Sukhoi logo on the tail and a playing cards diamond on the external tanks. The chained dog motive was created by one of the pilots of the regiment and subsequently applied on both the single- and two-seat Frogfoots operated by the 461st ShAP, with the first aircraft receiving it in 1998.

By mid-2012, there were about 50 upgraded Frogfoots reported in RuAF service, operated by two front-line attack aviation groups, as well as a few further examples serving with the aircrew combat training and conversion centre at Lipetsk and with the Flight Test Centre at Akhtubinsk.

In April 2012, the Russian ministry of defence announced that 80 additional Su-25s were slated for upgrade between 2012 and 2020; this way the total number of upgraded Su-25SMs in RuAF service will reach some 130 units for at least nine front-line squadrons.

The first upgraded and life-extended Su-25UBM two-seater took to the air for the first time on 11 December 2008 and, in 2009, another example joined the test and evaluation effort, which was eventually completed in December 2011 and took 85 successful sorties.

The enhanced Su-25SM3 is the definitive upgrade standard for the RuAF Frogfoot fleet and was tested for the first time in 2011. It added a host of further improvements, including a new mission computer, rendering the aircraft compatible with the newest digital weapons in RuAF service, such as the satellite-guided bombs, opening up new attack profiles in poor weather. It is believed that the SM3 standard was also made capable of deploying the KAB-500Kr TV-guided bomb and the Kh-29T TV-guided missile, and that an all-new communication system (including equipment for encrypted communication), IFF and video recording system were introduced.

The Su-25SM3 also boasted the Vitebsk-25 self-protection system, with a two-pod L-370-3S digital jammer system (accommodated on the two outermost wing hardpoints, previously used to carry R-60 air-to-air missiles) covering the frequency band from 7 to 10 GHz in a bid to bolster its self-protection capability, and was described as being much faster than the previous-generation analogue systems. The Vitebsk-25 also included a new directional infrared jammer system for the aircraft's rear and lower hemisphere, operating in conjunction with Reagent ultraviolet missile approach warners. The 1,100lb (500kg) KAB-500S satellite/INS-guided bomb was seen for the first time carried by an Su-25SM in early 2012, operated by the 929th State Flight Test Centre at Akhtubinsk.

This most capable avionics upgrade configuration is to be introduced in the production phase of the new-build Su-25UBM two-seaters and the upgrade of the existing Su-25s, while all the existing Su-25SMs (upgraded prior to 2012) are slated to be brought to the SM3 standard during their next main overhaul in the second half of the decade.

Su-25K Scorpion

The most radical Su-25 upgrade package yet announced was the Su-25KM Scorpion offered by Elbit Systems of Israel, a company well known for its very aggressive market approach to the upgrades of ex-Soviet platforms, which has established successful co-operation with the original Frogfoot production plant TAM of Georgia. The joint venture's aim was to produce a 'digitalized' and 'Westernized' derivative of the Su-25 and the Elbit/TAM upgrade package; named Scorpion, this was developed during late 2000 and early 2001. The technology demonstrator aircraft designated the Su-25KM (KM standing for Komercheski, Modernized – Commercial Upgrade), wearing Georgian military insignia and the serial '01', was flown for the first time on 18 April 2001 by Yehuda Shafir, Elbit's chief test pilot.

The Su-25K Scorpion is an enhanced Frogfoot derivative with a digital avionics suite offered by TAM of Georgia and Elbit Systems of Israel. (Author)

The Su-25KM's new avionics suite, featuring an all-new 'glass' cockpit, was developed around Elbit's Multi-role Modular Computer (MMRC), controlling dual Mil Std 1553 databases – one responsible for navigation and the other for the weapons delivery system. Precise navigation capability was provided thanks to a laser-gyro INS/GPS hydride system.

NATO and ICAO-compatible navaids – VOR/ILS and DME (TACAN optional) – were added, as were two new radios (one working in UHF and one in the VHF band) and a digital map generator.

Elbit's Display And Sight Helmet (DASH) was also offered to improve considerably the pilot's situation awareness. The DASH was reported to have been integrated to both the R-73 air-to-air missile and the new navigation system for marking points of interest on the ground during strike or reconnaissance missions. Complete mission pre-planning capability was also included in the core package.

Some of the original Russian-made instruments were retained on the Su-25KM, such as the SPO-15LM radar warning receiver (RWR), RV-15 radar altimeter, AoA indicator, engine RPM and fuel meter. New weapons that the Su-25KM could employ included the above-mentioned R-73 air-to-air missile (also manufactured by TAM) as well as Elbit's infrared-guided Opher and laser-guided Lizard bombs.

An aggressive marketing campaign, which was initiated by Elbit in 2001 and continued into 2002, was aimed at a number of existing European and Third World Frogfoot operators. In the event, the Su-25KM reported limited success, as the Georgian Air Force decided to upgrade four of its aircraft, while the prototype is believed to have been sold out to Turkmenistan; another Su-25KM was purchased by Gambia in 2003.

Su-25UB for SEAD

The 558th ARP, an aircraft repair plant, stationed in Baranovichi in Belarus and working in close cooperation with Sukhoi Attack Aircraft Company, has already undertaken a little-publicized upgrade of two Belarusian Air Force and two Peruvian Air Force Su-25UBs, for use in the demanding Suppression of Enemy Air Defence (SEAD) role. These Frogfoot-Bs received a new avionics package comprising the L150 Pastel radar warning receiver/emitter locator system, with most of its black boxes – together with the launch control and target designation equipment of the Kh-58U/E Anti-Radar Missile (ARM) – housed in a KRK-UO underfuselage pod. The rear cockpit instrument panel was transformed, adding an IM-3M-14 monochrome CRT display, onto which target and launch control information, derived from the Pastel and the seeker heads of the ARMs, was displayed. Data, comprising range, bearing and probable type of the enemy emitter, for up to six radars operating in the frequency between 1.2 and 18 GHz, could be displayed on the CRT, together with cues for launching the Kh-58U/E ARM, which boasted launch distances of between 4.3 and 54nm (8 and 100km).

Su-25M1/UBM1 upgrade in Ukraine

The single-seat Su-25M1 and the two-seat Su-25UBM1 represented a simplified and low-cost upgrade standard adopted by the Ukrainian Air Force and has been in testing since the mid-2000s. The main contractor for the upgrade was MiGremont company of Zaporozhye, a specialized aircraft repair plant, while all the components of the newly integrated avionics package were supplied by Ukrainian companies. The M1 standard was designed to replace a number of important components of the Su-25's original KN-23-1 navigation suite and the SUO-8-1 attack suite, improving the navigation and weapons delivery accuracy. Furthermore, to keep the cost as low as possible, no fuselage and powerplant alterations have been introduced, nor changes to the cockpit layout or equipment.

The list of the upgrade package's principal components included the new ILS-39 digital weapons sight and the SN-3307 GPS receiver, integrated with the existing KN-23-1 navigation suite; this novelty also enabled the Su-25M1 to perform the so-called navigational (non-visual) bombing against invisible targets with known position, achieving preciseness in the region of 100 to 160ft (30 to 50m). In addition, the new digitalized weapons sight enabled weapons delivery from higher altitudes – up to 19,800ft (6,000m) – and was advertized as having demonstrated some 30 per cent improved accuracy in comparison to the Su-25's original sighting equipment. Other components found in the Ukrainian upgrade package included a new air data system with digital output, new radio and the Karat digital flight data recorder. The arsenal of the upgraded Ukrainian Frogfoots was expanded with the S-13 122mm rocket fired from five-round B13 pods.

The Su-25M1/UBM1 standard was formally commissioned in Ukrainian service on 16 March 2010, with the first three upgraded and refurbished examples – two Su-25M1s and one Su-25UBM1 – taken on strength by the 209th Attack Aviation Brigade, stationed at Nikolaev-Kulbakino. In November 2011, two more upgraded single-seaters followed suit and, in 2012, another was taken on strength. In addition to the Ukrainian air arm, two Su-25UBs upgraded to a similar standard were delivered to Equatorial Guinea during 2007, and two single-seaters to the Democratic Republic of Congo followed in 2012.

There have been announcements suggesting that as many as 16 upgraded Frogfoots are slated to be taken on strength by 2016 by the Ukrainian Air Force.

OPERATIONAL HISTORY

Afghanistan

During Operation *Romb* in Afghanistan in 1980, the Su-25 underwent its field evaluation and testing effort in real-world combat conditions, as it was considered an integral part of the aircraft's comprehensive state testing and evaluation programme. In this way, the promising Frogfoot received its baptism of fire just five years following its maiden flight. Two prototypes, the first and third, designated the T8-1D and the T8-3 respectively, were deployed to Shindand airfield in Afghanistan on 18 April 1980, less than six months

after the Soviet invasion. The flight crews involved in Operation *Romb* included two test pilots from Sukhoi and two drawn from the Soviet Air Force's Flight Test Centre at Akhtubinsk (Vladimirovka).

The first familiarization flights in Afghan skies were logged on 21 April 1980. Initially, only evaluation sorties were flown, in order to explore the accuracy performance of the aircraft's signing system and weapons. The activity of the group, however, was not restricted to evaluation sorties, and the Su-25 was used in anger on 29 April, merely 11 days after its arrival, providing CAS to the Soviet land forces fighting *mujahedeen* (Afghan armed opposition fighters) in the province. During the evaluation period of 50 days of Operation *Romb*, the two Su-25 prototypes reportedly amassed 56 evaluation and 44 real-world combat sorties, logging in the process 98 hours and 11 minutes of total flight time. Of these sorties, 30 were considered within the frame of the type's state testing and evaluation effort. All the evaluation sorties were completed by 16 May, which, in turn, allowed the aircraft to fly real-world combat sorties until 5 June 1980. Among the achievements reported during Operation *Romb* were combat sorties flown with a maximum combat load of eight 1,100lb FAB-500 high-explosive bombs, as well as 32 220lb (100kg) OFAB-100 fragmentation/high explosive bombs.

The weapons used during the evaluation and combat sorties included 57mm, 80mm, 240mm and 250mm rockets, and 100kg, 250kg and 500kg free-fall bombs, as well as the RBK-250-275 cluster bombs. BetAB-500 concrete-penetration bombs were also employed on several occasions.

Among the Su-25's most notable strengths demonstrated during the experimental operation were the type's excellent hot-and-high performance and good aiming preciseness. Sukhoi test pilot Alexander Ivanov, who participated in Operation *Romb*, recalled:

> The 500kg bombs, when dropped by the Su-25, usually impacted within 30ft [10m] from the position of the sight's reticule placed on the target. The aircraft proved well capable of performing aerobatics with 2,200lb [1,000kg] of combat load and demonstrated benign handling behaviour in this configuration. The remarkable weapons delivery effectiveness of the Su-25s was also acknowledged by the ground forces.

The 80th OShaP was formed in early 1981 and immediately began work-up for its combat deployment to Afghanistan, as its initial cadre of pilots had just graduated from their conversion-to-type training on the Frogfoot at the VVS' Lipetsk-based 4th Combat Training and Aircrew Conversion Centre. (Andrey Zinchuk)

Among the aircraft's shortcomings noted by the test pilots during Operation *Romb* were the slow response of the R-95Sh engine and the low effectiveness of the petal-type airbrakes installed onto engine nacelles. In addition, the ASP-17BTs-8 electro-optical sight caused some issues in the beginning – it was not properly tuned to operate in mountainous conditions, despite most of the Su-25's targets being located at elevations high above sea level. This resulted in significant sighting errors, but the shortcoming was rapidly fixed.

Operation *Exam*

The successful experimental deployment of the Su-25 contributed greatly to the type's accelerated induction in regimental service with the VVS, since the new type clearly demonstrated that it was much more suitable for the CAS role in Afghanistan than any other front-line jet type in the Soviet Air Force inventory at the time. The first combat unit of the rejuvenated attack aviation arm of the Soviet Air Force's frontal aviation branch was the 80th OShaP, assigned to the Trans-Caucasus Military District. Formed in early 1981, it was stationed in Sital-Chai in today's Azerbaijan and took on strength its first Su-25s in April the same year.

The dedicated combat unit established for permanent deployment to Afghanistan was designated the 200th OShAE (Independent Attack Squadron). It was an independent front-line squadron, also formed at Sital-Chai in April–June 1981, on the base of the 80th OShAP, and received a fleet of 12 aircraft. The squadron deployed to Shindand airfield in Afghanistan on 19 July 1981, together with a team of engineers and technicians from the industry tasked to support the effort. The operation was code-named Operation *Exam* and was considered the formal operational testing effort for the type in real-world combat conditions. The first combat sorties of 200th OShAE were reportedly flown on 25 July. The main task of the squadron was to support the counter-insurgency operations of the Soviet Army's 5th Motorized Rifle Division, operating around Shindand, providing on-demand CAS and delivering strikes against pre-planned targets.

At the start of the Su-25's use in anger in Afghanistan, the 57mm S-5 rockets were employed but, due to their insufficient destructive power, they were promptly superseded by the much more powerful 80mm rockets of the S-8 family. (Author's collection)

In 1982, the area of operations of the 200th OShAE was significantly expanded and this was reflected in the workload, which sharply increased. The Su-25s were called upon to bomb targets in other regions in Afghanistan, including the capital Kabul and the hot zones around Bagram and Kandahar. Pilots often flew four to five sorties a day, and there were some quite intense days when they amassed up to eight sorties.

The first shift of air and ground crews of the squadron – the so-called first personnel rotation – ended its in-theatre deployment in October 1982 with no losses reported. All the pilots and technicians of the unit were replaced by new ones, also drawn from the 80th OShAP. As many as 2,000 combat sorties were logged during the first personnel rotation and on 12 occasions the squadron's Su-25s returned to the base with one engine inoperative due to combat damage from small-arms fire. During the first eight months of operation, each Su-25 in theatre averaged 178 flying hours.

All the Su-25 missions were flown with a pair of 800l external tanks under the wings in order to extend the otherwise limited range and endurance. Without external tanks, the Su-25 was restricted to operate against targets at a maximum radius

The outcome of the operations of the 200th OShAE's first personnel rotation proved to be very positive, as the aircraft used its unmatched agility to full extent for manoeuvring into narrow mountain valleys and precisely delivering its ordnance, something that was impossible for the Soviet fighter-bombers deployed to Afghanistan. (Andrey Zinchuk)

of 108nm (200km) from the base. The ordnance that was typically carried on long-range sorties, when using drop tanks at a radius of up to 161nm (300km) from the base, included two to four bombs or rocket packs, while the combat load for the cannon was reduced from 250 to 150–170 rounds.

There were some stringent operational restrictions imposed on the 200th OShAE's Su-25 in the beginning, mainly caused by the aircraft's unreliable navigation equipment and, as a consequence, the Frogfoot was not permitted to participate in combat operations in bad weather or during the night in the first years of the war. Furthermore, the intense combat operations revealed a few serious design shortcomings, such as the low reliability of the ARK-15 ADF and the RSBN-6 short-range aid to navigation. Both of these navigation aids proved ill-suited for operation in mountain conditions due to the lack of line-of-sight between the ground transmitters and the aircraft during low-level flight. Both of the systems demonstrated poor reliability even when operating over flat terrain, and this particular shortcoming forced Frogfoot drivers to rely on the old and tried navigation method with maps, magnetic compass and stopwatch.

The strengths of the Su-25's ground servicing included the rapid pre-flight preparation and suspension of weapons; the time necessary for pre-flight of a four-ship flight accounted for 25 minutes only, while an eight-ship mission required 40 minutes of pre-flight work. It is noteworthy that this turnaround time was achieved by means of manual work operations, without using any forklifts or other sophisticated mechanization, ground support equipment or specialized tools.

Initially, the S-5 57mm rockets were used, fired from the UB-32-57 32-round packs, but it was rapidly discovered that these simple and lightweight rockets had rather low destructive power when used in mountain conditions. That is why the 57mm rockets were rapidly replaced by the much more powerful S-8 80mm rockets, fired from 20-round B-8M packs. Use of the S-8 was most effective against area targets in plain areas and the most lethal versions against manpower on open terrain proved to be the S-8D and S-8M derivatives, fitted with thermobaric warheads to create a powerful blast.

The 1,100lb (500kg) ODAB-500 thermobaric bombs were also commonly used weapons against manpower in the open or hiding in shelters, trenches or mountain caves. Due to the

A variation of the Gratch (rook) badge, widely introduced from 1984 in Afghanistan, which eventually provided the Su-25's unofficial and rather popular campaign nickname. (Andrey Zinchuk archive)

powerful blast – said to be three times more powerful than that of the high-explosive bombs with the same weight – the ODAB-500 bomb was also widely used to clear minefields and for preparing the areas for pre-planned helicopter-borne assault landing parties.

The S-24 240mm rockets were mainly used for destroying point targets due to their remarkably high precision and the powerful high-explosive/fragmentation warhead weighing 270lb (123kg). The S-24 was later supplemented by the S-25OFM, which boasted a far more lethal warhead, suitable for use against hardened targets.

The main types of bombs used in Afghanistan were the OFAB-100 and OFAB-250 of fragmentation/high-explosive type, as well as the more powerful FAB-500-M56 or -M62 and the RBK-250 and RBK-500 cluster bombs. Another commonly employed weapon was the ZAB-500 napalm canister for attacking area targets.

The GSh-30 built-in cannon was regarded as a last-ditch weapon and was rarely used in combat while the podded GSh-23L in forward- and rearward-firing SPPU-22-01 pods was a more frequently employed cannon.

In addition to the usual on-demand CAS and pre-planned strikes, the Su-25 was also widely used for aerial mine-laying missions, as well as for the escort of helicopter groups during large-scale assault operations and of ground vehicle convoys, special operations forces support, search and destroy operations (i.e. free-style hunting operations) against the *mujahedeen* supply routes and day/night patrolling over the airfields to prevent rocket and mortar attacks and provide cover (against hand-held SAM launches) for take-offs and landings of large transport aircraft. Use of the Su-25 for visual reconnaissance was undertaken on rare occasions and at low altitude, mainly pre- and post-strike.

The call sign of the Su-25 formations, used by the forward air controllers during the war in Afghanistan was 'Grach' (rook) – this was the chief reason the aircraft came to be nicknamed 'The Grach' from 1984. As a result, cartoon rook badges in a large number of variations started to appear on many Su-25s deployed to Afghanistan and later the rook became commonplace on the Soviet and Russian Air Force Su-25 single-seaters.

The first Su-25 loss in Afghanistan happened during the second rotation of the 200th OShAE – from October 1982 to October 1983 – and it was not related to combat damage circumstances; instead this loss was caused by one of the Su-25's inherent shortcomings, namely the poor controllability in bank due to the excessively high stick forces induced by the manually-actuated ailerons. In this sortie, the pilot, Capt Mikhail Dyakov, proved unable to counter the violent unintentional banking caused by the non-symmetrical 1,100lb (500kg) bomb separation in dive attack. As a consequence, his uncontrollable aircraft failed to pull out from the dive and impacted the

E   **A SOVIET Su-25 ATTACKS A *MUJAHEDEEN* CAMP, 1988**

A Soviet Air Force Su-25 seen performing attacks on a *mujahedeen* camp in Afghanistan by employing FAB-500ShN retarded bombs released at low altitude. Most of the pre-planned attacks of the Frogfoot force in Afghanistan were made in the early morning hours, using the element of surprise while approaching from the side of the rising sun. Low-level attacks were rare during the second half of the campaign, especially after 1987, as these were allowed only in special cases because of the sharply increased Stinger SAM treat. After releasing the ordnance, the pilots were required to initiate pull-up immediately, while completing defensive manoeuvring by sharply turning left and right and maintaining a 30-degree climb. Flares were pumped from the moment of releasing the ordnance until reaching the safe altitude of around 19,800ft (6,000m) above terrain.

ground, killing the pilot. This crash prompted an urgent Frogfoot modification by means of the introduction of hydraulic actuators for the ailerons, which increased the maximum speed limit to 540kt (1,000km/h), while the maximum G-limit was also increased to 6.5 units. The newly built Su-25s also received better airbrakes, preventing acceleration in diving attacks, dual-redundant nosewheel steering and improved fuel system and engines with longer life. The whole package of improvements, based on the initial operational experience, was incorporated on the aircraft of the 5th Series production standard.

The third personnel rotation with the 200th OShAE began in October 1983, still deploying the original 1st Series Su-25s delivered in 1981. During the 12-month deployment, until October 1984, two Frogfoot losses were reported. The first of these was again unrelated to enemy action, with the pilot ejecting safely. The second, however, claimed the life of 200th OShAE squadron commander, Lt Col Peter Ruban; during a bombing run his aircraft took numerous hits from ground fire that inflicted serious damage to the control system and the engines.

In early 1984, the 200th OShAE saw permanent redeployment to Bagram airfield and its next personnel rotation, in September–October, saw new air and ground crews coming from the second Soviet Air Force attack regiment that converted to the type – the 90th OShAP, stationed at Artsiz in Ukraine. They deployed from the Soviet Union with brand new 6th Series Su-25s, which in the beginning were used alongside the worn-out 1st Series aircraft, the latter being gradually replaced upon their TBO expiry (set at 800 flight hours).

378th OShAP enters the theatre

On 8 October 1984 – just two weeks after the arrival of the personnel of the next rotation with the 200th OShAE – a brand new attack aircraft unit was purposely established for operations in Afghanistan: the 378th OShAP (Independent Attack Aviation Regiment), stationed at Bagram. Set on the base of the 200th OShAE, initially it was a two-squadron attack regiment with a total complement of 28 Su-25s; 12 in each squadron plus four further Frogfoots assigned to the regiment's command flight. The pilots and technicians of the newly formed attack regiment were drawn from the two existing Soviet Air Force Frogfoot front-line regiments at the time, the 80th and the 90th OShAPs.

The high intensity of the combat operations performed over the entire territory of Afghanistan resulted in almost 11,000 combat sorties being amassed in one year by the two squadrons of the 378th OShAP, between October 1984 and October 1985. Most of the CAS sorties were performed from altitudes of 1,960 to 3,280ft (600 to 1,000m) above terrain, thanks to the aircraft's decent armour protection, providing reliable resistance to the small-arms fire from the ground. Dropping bombs and firing rockets from such low altitudes resulted in accurate hits, making the Su-25 a deadly CAS asset. There were 12 occasions when the 378th OShaP's Frogfoots returned to the base on one engine as a result of combat damage of varying degrees that had forced the pilots to switch off the other engine. During its first personnel rotation, the 378th OShAP reported two aircraft and their pilots lost in action; in addition, it suffered from two more non-combat-related losses. The average number of sorties per aircraft in this period was 216, while the maximum number reached 315.

Lt Col Grigorii Strepetov, a prominent Shturmovik pilot, was CO of the 2nd Squadron of the 378th OShAP during his 1986–87 combat employment to Afghanistan. (Author's collection – Aviatsia i Kosmonavtika)

LT COL ALEXANDER RUTSKOI'S UNEASY COMBAT CAREER

The 378th OShAP CO during the second rotation period was Lt Col Alexander Rutskoi, widely known as a prominent leader but also described as a reckless attack pilot, who always tried to exploit the full extent of the aircraft's combat capabilities and often ventured beyond them for too long. From the beginning of his career in Afghanistan, Rutskoi flew combat sorties in a very aggressive manner and twice returned with fire onboard; on one of those occasions his aircraft sustained no less than 39 bullet hits. He had to overcome numerous challenges and troubles during his two combat deployments in Afghanistan, including two shoot-downs with subsequent ejections, both of which he barely survived.

It was not surprising that, during the second 378th OShAP personnel rotation, the first combat loss was the aircraft of the regimental CO, Lt Col Rutskoi. His Su-25 was gunned down by the combined fire of a shoulder-launched missile and anti-aircraft artillery on 6 April 1986 during a large low-level attack against the Djavara *mujahedeen* base. The pilot ejected successfully from very low altitude and high bank angle, sustaining serious back injuries and a broken arm upon landing. Following a prolonged recovery period, Rutskoi returned to Afghanistan in April in 1988 – already promoted to colonel and appointed deputy commander (aviation) of Soviet's 40th Army – to continue flying and fighting the *mujahedeen* in the same reckless style and even more aggressively than before. He had the bad luck to be gunned down again on 4 August 1988, this time by an AIM-9L Sidewinder air-to-air missile fired by a Pakistani Air Force F-16A, scrambled from Kamra (piloted by Sqn Ldr Athar Bokhari). Ironically, this happened in the same border area he had been downed in two years before, near Djavara, close to the border city of Khost. He landed well inside Pakistani territory, was taken prisoner of war and subsequently released two weeks later, thanks to the great efforts of the Soviet Government and its intelligence services.

Colonel Alexander Rutskoi, a prominent Shturmovik pilot and commander, who underwent two ejections in combat operations during the Afghanistan campaign. (Author's collection)

Between 20 September 1984 and 1 January 1985, the Su-25s operating in Afghanistan logged 1,600 hours, reporting some 171 failures. Mean time between failures (MTBF) in respect of the failures found during ground checks was 11 hours, and in respect of the failures occurring during flight was 62.5 hours.

The second personnel rotation that began in October 1985 saw the expansion of the 378th OShAP structure to three squadrons – each with 12 aircraft plus four more assigned to the regiment's command flight. Two of the squadrons and the command section were based at Bagram, while the third was stationed at Kandahar.

Guided missile strikes

In 1986, the 378th OshAP's Su-25s commenced flying night combat sorties and the pilots also began mastering the daytime employment of the Kh-25ML and Kh-29L laser-guided missiles, enabling stand-off strikes against high-value point targets from up to 4.3nm (8km). The first laser-guided missile missions by the Su-25 were reported in April 1986, for attacking the entrances of a number of caves used as shelters and weapons storage facilities within the confines of the well-hardened Djavara base, next to the border with Pakistan. Guidance of the missiles was initially provided by the Su-25's Klyon-PS laser designator/rangefinder, but this was said to have proved difficult because of system tuning issues and a lack of auto-tracking capability. Consequently, in 1987, the BOMAN laser-designation vehicle was introduced by the 378th OShAP. It was a makeshift targeting system, based on the body of a BTR-80

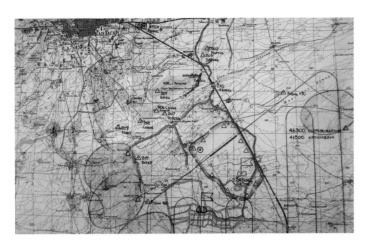

A Soviet Air Force combat operations map of Kandahar area, at the time known to be a very troubled place, where the 3rd squadron of the 376th OShAP – stationed at Kandahar airfield – operated until its withdrawal in late 1988. (Author's collection)

armoured personnel carrier, equipped with the Klyon-PS system (scavenged from an Su-25 damaged beyond repair) that was optically aimed, using the sight of a 12.7mm machine gun. According to data released by Sukhoi, as many as 139 laser-guided missiles were launched by the 378th OShAP Su-25s during the Afghanistan war campaign, using its own Klyon-PS or a BOMAN vehicle for target lasing.

The night combat sorties flown by the 378th OShAP Frogfoots necessitated employment of the SAB-100 or SAB-250 illumination bombs, carried by one aircraft in the four-ship flight. After dropping the illumination bombs, which slowly descended with parachutes, the other three Su-25s attacked the visually distinguishable target with bombs and rockets from shallow dive.

Between October 1985 and October 1986, the 378th OShAP flew as many as 24,157 combat sorties, logged in the course of 5,343 ground attack, escort and reconnaissance missions. Each pilot had between 270 and 300 combat hours under his belt, while each Frogfoot in theatre logged between 250 and 300 sorties, averaging 224 hours. The 378th OShAP fleet suffered from a total of 72 different in-flight combat damages during the same period – 54 of these caused by small arms projectiles and 18 more from missile warhead fragments. Eight aircraft were reported lost in action, and a few further examples were damaged beyond repair during emergency landings or as a result of the heavy combat damage, mostly caused by shoulder-launched surface-to-air missiles (SAMs).

No less than five Su-25s downed during this period were brought down by the *mujahedeen*'s shoulder-launched SAMs, represented at the time by the FIM-43 Red Eye and the Strela-2M (SA-7 Grail), introduced to mass use by the *mujahedeen* in 1984.

Two pilots were lost during this personnel rotation period, as both had little flying experience – one was killed during unsuccessful ejection from a heavily damaged Su-25, while the other was lost in unclear circumstances during a night sortie.

The protection against *mujahedeen*'s heat-seeking missiles was originally provided by four ASO-2V-01 flare dispensers, installed next to the tail fin and ejecting PPI-26 heat-emitting flares to decoy the SAMs, as their heat-seeking guidance systems were prone to high-temperature flare jamming. The dispensers, however, were deemed ill-suited to prolonged use during multiple attacks since they contained only 126 flares; furthermore, the control panel for flare ejection was installed on the starboard panel in the cockpit, which was not easy for the pilot to access during attack runs. The prompt measures for improving the Su-25's self-protection against heat-seeking, handheld SAMs – undertaken by Sukhoi – called for scabbing four additional ASO-2V-01 dispensers onto the upper side of the engine nacelles; this increased the flare capacity from 128 to 256. The eight 32-round dispenser units enabled the Su-25 to mount as many as eight attacks by pumping flares in a pre-set sequence. The first modified Frogfoots, featuring an increased number of ASO-2V dispensers and automatic flare pumping programming, were adapted on-site in Afghanistan in early 1986.

The year of heaviest losses

The third personnel rotation with the 378th OShAP, taking place from October 1986 to October 1987, involved pilots gathered from all three existing Su-25-equipped front-line attack regiments in the Soviet Union at the time: the 80th, 90th and 368th OShAPs. They were deployed to the war theatre just in time to face a new, far more lethal threat, as the *mujahedeen* started using the modern FIM-82A Stinger shoulder-launched SAM, which had considerably better resistance to jamming by flares. The mass introduction of the Stinger proved to be a decisive factor enabling *mujahedeen* field commanders to effectively counter the threat posed by the low-flying Soviet ground attack jets and helicopters.

In addition to the jam resistance and more precise guidance, the Stinger boasted longer reach, a more powerful warhead and a proximity fuse for increased kill probability. In the period between November 1986 and February 1987, no fewer than four Su-25s were gunned down using this deadly weapon.

The 1986–87 personnel rotation at the 378th OShAP reported the highest combat attrition rate of the war campaign, accounting for eight Su-25s and five pilots, while no fewer than three further Frogfoots were reported lost in accidents or damaged beyond economical repair and subsequently dismantled for spares or sent back to the Soviet Union for combat damage analyses. This way, the 40-aircraft 378th OShAP lost no less than 35 per cent of its fleet in only one year of intense counter-insurgency combat operations against a well-armed and motivated enemy.

One of the Su-25s lost during this period, piloted by Capt M. Burak, is believed to have been shot down by a direct hit of a 122mm illumination round, fired by the Soviet artillery unit above *mujahedeen* positions attacked by Frogfoots, killing the pilot. Three more pilots from the 378th OShAP were lost in non-combat-related accidents, and the only confirmed combat loss was Lt Konstanin Pavlukov; he was gunned down by a Stinger SAM immediately following take-off from Bagram in December 1986, ejecting successfully but then killed as a hero on the ground in a fierce firefight with the *mujahedeen*.

Major Anatoliy Obedkov was among three very lucky pilots who managed to perform emergency landings with their heavily damaged Su-25s. The event took place when a Stinger hit the fuselage and engine during a low-level ground convoy attack mission in an eight-ship formation on 28 July 1987:

> The SAM scored a hit next to my port engine, shredding the nacelle, the upper part of the combustion chamber and jamming the low-pressure turbine. The fragments from the detonated warhead damaged both DC converters and with an electrical system lost, it proved impossible to jettison the bombs under the wing; the only working instruments in the cabin were the vertical speed indicator and the airspeed indicator. Furthermore, the ravaging fire in the DC converters area caused overheating of a wiring bundle

In the beginning of the war, the Su-25s performed four- and eight-ship attacks in multiple shallow dive passes, while, in the late stage from early 1987, the main method of performing attack runs was in a steep dive from high altitude, pulling up at 14,850ft (4,500m). (Andrey Zinchuk)

located next to the converters, resulting in a series of short circuits. These short circuits, in turn, led to unintentional deployment of my braking chute in flight at a speed of around 189kt [350km/h] and the chute failed to separate immediately after that. So, I decided to commence immediate descent and look what will happen with the deployed chute in this uneasy situation. Luckily, it went away at last, but seeing the deployed chute falling to the ground prompted the other seven pilots in my group to think that I have ejected. After separation, the twin-dome chute descended for 160ft (50m) and then both the domes suddenly collapsed as it fell right away onto the ground. As it could be guessed, all the pilots in the formation escorting me thought I was killed in my ejection attempt due to the parachute failure. I, however, managed to stay aloft and get my damaged plane to Kabul; due to the severe buffeting I decided to attempt landing there. The heavily damaged and burning Su-25 with damaged controls touched down, but without operative brakes and brake chute; as a result it rolled through the entire length of the runway at a high speed, overshot and continued moving onto the ground, stopping at last in trench next to a mine field.

Major Obedkov's 8th Series Su-25 – serialled '23', c/n 08033 – was hit by one of two Stingers, which created a hole 3ft high and 5ft long (1m by 1.6m) onto the starboard side. In addition to the lost electrical system, the severe damage caused a complete failure of the aircraft's dual-redundant hydraulic system. The fire onboard was fed by the flammable hydraulic fluid spraying under pressure from the torn lines, while the control runs also suffered badly from heat damage. As discovered after the landing, some 95 per cent of the control rod diameter had been eaten by the fire. The system remained operative until the end of this very dramatic sortie, however. As Maj Obedkov recalled later, after the hit, his heavily laden Frogfoot – carrying two 800l drop tanks under the wings, four RBK-250 550lb cluster bombs, two full B-8M rocket packs and 3,000l of fuel onboard – continued flying at a speed as low as 92kt (170km/h), gradually accelerating to 151kt (280km/h) and even climbing with one engine inoperative. This particular aircraft was later handed over to Sukhoi for a detailed examination of the damage inflicted by the Stinger hit and an evaluation of the effectiveness of the self-protection features implemented on 8th Series aircraft.

A view of the Su-25's engine after close detonation of a Stinger SAM during an experiment performed by the Sukhoi Design Bureau in 1987 or 1988. (Sukhoi Company)

Combat survivability enhancements

In an effort to boost the combat damage resistance in case of close detonation of a Stinger missile, in early 1987 Sukhoi introduced a set of urgent design improvement measures. These included a 5ft (1.5m) long, 5mm thick armour plate situated between the engines, fire insulation blankets to prevent damage from one engine to the other, as well as a new inert gas fire extinguisher system consisting of fire warning sensors in the engine nacelles and six bottles with Freon neutral gas, manually activated in two stages by the pilot. New steel control rods for better resistance to fire were also added, along with additional armour protection for vital systems. The weight of the armour and fire protection increased by 770lb (350kg), reaching a total of 2,420lb (1,100kg). The enhanced-protection Su-25s, built to the 9th Series production standard, were introduced in Afghanistan for the first time in August 1987; it is also noteworthy that a number of the last 8th Series aircraft built also received this extensive set of combat survivability enhancements.

In addition to the urgent design measures for enhancing the Su-25's combat survivability, there were also significant changes introduced in the 378th OShAP tactics, aimed at reducing the aircraft's vulnerability from SAM and AAA fire. It called for performing attacks from high altitude, which, however, reduced the preciseness and therefore the effectiveness of the CAS operation. During pre-planned strike missions, the Su-25 pilots were ordered to enter into steep diving attack runs for bomb drops from 23,100 to 26,400ft (7,000 to 8,000m) and even 29,700ft (9,000m), while minimum altitude to commence climb-out after releasing the ordnance was required to be no lower than 14,850ft (4,500m).

There were some other issues caused by the transition to high-altitude operations, such as the frequent health problems reported by the Frogfoot pilots due to the aircraft's non-pressurized cockpit; they suffered from the rapid changes in the atmospheric pressure and the frequent use of pure oxygen for breathing. In addition, in a bid to reduce the loss rate, since late 1985 the 378th OShAP Su-25s had begun to undertake intense night operations, mostly by attacking targets with known position or upon targeting instructions received by forward air controllers.

There were a few exceptions for mounting attacks below 14,850ft (4,500m), as these were permitted only in a few cases – for example, CAS provided to special operation forces or motorized infantry units in contact with the enemy, combat SAR operations to rescue downed aircrews, as well as for attacking ground convoys of vehicles and animals that ferried supplies and weapons from Pakistan or Iran.

The cautious approach to combat – with the combination of high-altitude day and night attack sorties – was said to have sharply reduced the number of losses in 1988. In fact, the only combat loss reported in the period was the Frogfoot flown by Col Rutskoi, downed by the Pakistani F-16 on 4 August as described previously. Two further Su-25s were written off due to non-combat-related causes, while eight more were destroyed on the ground during an artillery and rocket attack against Kabul airport on 23 June 1988; another Su-25 saw the same fate at Kandahar.

The Soviet occupation of Afghanistan ended in February 1989 and only one aircraft from the last rotation – deployed from October 1988 to February 1989 – was reported lost in combat. The last deployment reported 4,157 combat sorties in four months of operations to support the inglorious withdrawal of the Soviet military units from Afghanistan.

The Afghan war in summary

In total, the Soviet AF Su-25s amassed more than 60,000 combat sorties in Afghanistan until the withdrawal in February 1989. The Frogfoot handled the intense in-theatre combat workload well, comprising up to six sorties a day and backed by little or no maintenance in the field.

Combat-related Frogfoot losses during the campaign, according to official information released by Sukhoi, were quoted as 23 aircraft gunned down and 12 pilots killed in action. In fact, some independent research on the Su-25 operations and analysis of numerous pilot narratives tended to show that only half of this number of pilots was actually killed in action by enemy fire, while the rest were killed as a consequence of handling mistakes, equipment failures or even friendly fire. Between 1984 and 1988, as many as 163 SAM launches were reported against the 378th OShAP Frogfoots, resulting in 12 hits that shot down their intended targets.

A dozen or so additional aircraft were believed to have been lost in non-combat-related accidents in Afghanistan, while another dozen were written off due to extensive combat damage or bad landings that rendered them beyond economical repair. No fewer than nine further Su-25s were also destroyed on the ground by enemy mortar and rocket fire at Kabul and Kandahar. In total, the losses in the air and on the ground during the campaign accounted for no fewer than 37 Su-25s and 12 pilots; there were additional aircraft that were damaged beyond repair and used as spare parts donors or for combat damage evaluation. According to the prominent researchers of the Soviet Air Force and its Afghanistan war operations, Viktor Markovskii and Igor Prikhodchenko, the Su-25's losses in Afghanistan represented some 25 per cent of the total Soviet Air Force fixed-wing losses reported during the nine-year campaign. The chief reason for such a high loss rate suffered by the Frogfoot force could be found in the very nature of its attack operations, since aircraft providing CAS at low altitude were considered prime targets for the *mujahedeen*'s shoulder-launched SAMs and AAA. A contributing cause for this significant loss rate is related to the large proportion of young and inexperienced lieutenants and senior lieutenants rushed into combat in Afghanistan, especially during the first and second personnel rotations with the 378th OShAP.

In fact, the Su-25's employment in Afghanistan as a real low-altitude attack aircraft – i.e. going into harm's way to provide CAS and destroy hardened targets on the battlefield – was somewhat limited after 1985. No less than 80 per cent of the combat sorties amassed during this protracted and slow-going counter-insurgency war, especially after 1985, were flown in a pure fighter-bomber style of operation, i.e. in large strike packages for knocking out pre-planned targets in rebel-held territory by dropping bombs and unleashing rockets from safe altitude in one diving run only.

The Russian Air Force Su-25s emerged in the early 1990s as the most useful and cost-effective combat jets, serving with no less than seven front-line attack regiments. Here, a late-production Frogfoot is seen armed with a Kh-25ML laser-guided air-to-surface missile. (Author's collection)

The Frogfoot in the post-Soviet wars

At the time just before the dissolution of the Soviet Union, the VVS frontal aviation branch had on strength as many as ten independent attack regiments (directly subordinated to the aviation command authorities of their respective military district or regional air army), equipped with the Frogfoot, each with two or three squadrons and command flight. The fleet of the three-squadron regiments comprised, as a rule, 40 single-seaters and four to six two-seaters.

In addition, the Su-25 was operated by no fewer than three dedicated training squadrons, one instructor attack regiment and one independent target-towing squadron. The Soviet naval aviation service also had on strength in the late 1980s as many as three independent attack regiments and a dedicated aircrew training and research squadron. The total number of Frogfoots of all versions in active service with the VVS and the naval aviation arm accounted for about 570 examples, including 96 two-seaters.

After the break-up of the Soviet Union, the newly independent states of Belarus and Ukraine inherited large Frogfoot fleets from the inventory of the VVS regiments previously based on their territory. The former received as many as 81 single-seaters and 19 two-seaters (equalling the entire fleet of three front-line attack regiments), while the latter had 92 aircraft of all variants (the entire fleet of two front-line attack regiments, one naval aviation attack regiment and one naval aviation training and research squadron).

In the post-Soviet era, the Su-25 saw operational use in a good many regional conflicts, the first of which was the war between Abkhazia and Georgia in 1993–94; the second involved Azerbaijan and Armenia in 1992–94 over the territory of Nagorni Karabakh; while the third was the Russian campaign mounted against the Islamic fundamentalists on the Tajikistan-Afghanistan border in 1993–94.

In the first two of these conflicts, both warring sides used the Frogfoot in anger. Azerbaijan, for instance, received its first Su-25 after it was hijacked on 8 April 1992 from the 80th OShAP in Sital-Chai by an Azeri pilot, Lt Vaghit Kurbanov. This aircraft was immediately put in use for bombing missions against the Armenian forces in the Nagorni Karabakh area and the capital Stepanakert, as well as in border zones on Armenian territory. Based at Evlakh in Azerbaijan, the lone Frogfoot continued flying for two months, until shot down by the Armenian forces on 13 June. After that, Azerbaijan purchased no fewer than five Su-25s from Georgia, which were rushed into combat in mid-1992, mainly for bombing Stepanakert and widely employing cluster and large-calibre high-explosive bombs. Four of these Frogfoots were eventually gunned down by the Armenian forces between October 1992 and April 1994.

Armenia also introduced the type in 1992, as it took delivery of seven Su-25s, including two two-seaters, as military aid provided by Russia. These also saw a great deal of use in anger until the end of hostilities in May 1994, bombing targets in Azerbaijan and on the front line in the Nagorni Karabakh area, with at least one Su-25 reported lost in action.

By late 1991, the total number of Frogfoots of all versions in active service with the Soviet Air Force and the naval aviation arm accounted for no fewer than about 570 examples. This weathered example belonged to the 18th Guards ShAP, named 'Normandie-Nieman', stationed at Galiyonki in Russia's Far East, which took part in the combat operations in Tajikistan. (Andrey Zinchuk collection)

The war between Georgia and the breakaway province of Abkhazia saw use of some eight Su-25s, operated by the newly established Georgian air arm. The aircraft, powered by the R-195 engines, were taken from the undelivered stocks at the Tbilisi aviation plant and saw use in anger for the first time in February 1993, bombing the Abkhazian forces stationed in the city of Gudauta and on the front line in the border area. As many as six Georgian Frogfoots were reported lost in combat (one of them by friendly fire) until the end of 1993. In the spring of the same year, Russian Air Force Su-25s deployed to Gudauta airfield joined the war on the Abkhazian side and performed a series of attacks against the Georgian forces positioned around the coastal city of Sukhumi.

The Russian Air Force's Su-25s were also rushed into combat in the conflict on the border between Tajikistan and Afghanistan. A squadron of Frogfoots, belonging to the 186th IShAP (Instructor Attack Regiment) from Buturlinovka in the central part of Russia, was urgently deployed to Kokaity airfield in Uzbekistan and immediately after arrival its Frogfoots began flying regular bombing sorties. Later on, personnel from the other RuAF attack regiments rotated on temporary deployments there, in order to ensure a long-term air power presence in the troubled region.

The main targets of the Russian Frogfoots during this little-known but fierce and rather bloody local conflict were Islamist rebel groups, entering into Tajikistan from Afghanistan by crossing the Pyandj river and then moving to fight inside the country through a number of mountain passes. The most intense year for fighting the Islamists proved to be 1994, with 116 strike and 171 reconnaissance sorties amassed by the deployed Su-25s, while the total flight time of the detachment accounted for 617 hours.

In late 1995, the group, consisting of 10 aircraft (six single-seaters and four two-seaters), moved to Dushanbe-Aini airfield in Tajikistan and continued its unsung combat work from there. Two Su-25s were reported to have been lost since the beginning of the deployment, in 1998 and 2005 respectively, but both of these were written off in non-combat-related accidents.

Chechnya

The next use in anger of the Russian Frogfoot units – by that time considered combat-hardened warriors – was when they were called into action in the breakaway Russian republic of Chechnya. There, three attack regiments were involved with a total fleet of more than 60 aircraft, operating mostly from Mozdok airfield in nearby Dagestan.

The total number of combat sorties amassed in both war campaigns, in 1994–95 and 1999–2000 respectively, exceeded 6,000. Three aircraft were reported to have been lost to enemy fire in the first war (mainly from the fire of 23mm anti-aircraft guns), while another five or six were lost either to enemy air defences or other causes – such as controlled flight into terrain in mountains in bad weather – during the second campaign.

During both Chechen campaigns, the RuAF Su-25s were employed mainly in the classic clear-weather, day-only 'bomb truck/flying rocket battery' role as the complex missions with guided weapons and in the night were carried out by the Su-24Ms and Su-25Ts. Most of the strikes were of pre-planned type, against targets with known position, and all bombing and rocket firings were performed using the ASP-17BTs-8 sight in manual aiming mode only. There was also a proportion of free hunting sorties – to destroy targets of opportunity – with the aircraft patrolling in assigned zones, as well as CAS sorties using a network of forward air controllers.

During the second Chechen campaign the Su-25s were employed mostly in four-ship flights. There was at least one occasion when they provided air support in bad weather in an emergency situation; this was to help airborne troops, ambushed by the Chechen insurgents near Ulus-Kert. They fired the heavy S-24 rockets below the cloud base while in climb in a bid to complete area saturation on a mountain slope above them that was always covered by dense clouds.

This shark-mouthed RuAF Su-25 – armed with 80mm rocket packs and wearing the traditional Gratch badge – was among the Frogfoots that fought against the Islamists in Tajikistan in the 1990s and early 2000s. (Andrey Zinchuk)

One of the most famous Frogfoot strike missions was performed four days before the launch of the second Chechen campaign in 1999, involving the aircraft of all three regiments, deployed to Mozdok. As many as 60 aircraft were scrambled in a single wave and complete radio silence was used to mount a devastating strike against a number of targets in Chechnya – mainly airfields and storage facilities with heavy military equipment – using rockets with armour-piercing warheads and high-explosive bombs.

Between late 1999 and mid-2000, two Su-25Ts drawn from the Lipetsk-based 4th TsPLSiBP (Aircrew Conversion and Combat Training Centre) were deployed to Mozdok; these were to be used for destroying a number of high-value targets in Chechnya, such as a satellite communications facility, radio relay station, the fortified house of the well-known Chechen field commander Shamil Bassaev, a hangar housing defence equipment and, curiously, an An-2 light transport biplane on the ground, suspected to be ferrying weapons from nearby Georgia. Kh-29L and Kh-25ML laser-guided missiles were the main types of weapons employed by the Su-25T pair in Chechnya, while the KAB-500L laser-guided and ODAB-500 1,100lb (500kg) free-fall fuel-air bombs were occasionally used to destroy underground shelters and weapons storage facilities.

The 2008 war in South Ossetia

The war in South Ossetia and Abkhazia in August 2008 was triggered by a Georgian mass attack launched in the late evening of 7 August 2008 against the tiny breakaway region of South Ossetia; both warring sides used the Frogfoot in the conflict.

The RuAF's 368th ShAP – an attack regiment of the 4th Air Army stationed in Budyonnovsk, not far from South Ossetia – received an alert order at midnight on 7 August. By the early hours of the next day its CO, Col Sergey Kobilash, was given a mission tasking his regiment directly from the RuAF commander-in-chief, Col Gen Alexander Zelin. The regiment was tasked to send two four-ship flights in an effort to provide much-needed air support to the Russian peacekeeping forces defending the South Ossetian capital of Tskhinvali.

The four Su-25s of the formation led by Col Kobilash were the first RuAF aircraft to appear over the battlefield around Tskhinvali. Using the element of surprise, the Frogfoots mounted devastating strafing passes against a Georgian vehicle column, unleashing 80mm rockets. The leaders of each pair in the Frogfoot formations flew the upgraded Su-25SM outfitted with far better sighting and navigation equipment, while their wingmen had ordinary (i.e. non-upgraded) Su-25s. The first air attack was described as having caused the

A Russian Air Force Su-25 four-ship flight seen in an ultra low-level pass over Mozdok airfield returning from a combat mission in the troubled republic of Chechnya during the first war (1994–96). (Andrey Zinchuk collection)

highest number of losses among the Georgian forces in the war, with 22 troops killed and many vehicles destroyed.

The Frogfoot force from Budyonnovsk continued flying CAS sorties around Tskhinvali in the late afternoon hours of this critical day and, at that time, the 368th ShAP suffered its first loss. It was an Su-25BM wearing serial '10', which was flown by Lt Col Oleg Terebunskyi. It took hits by shoulder-launched SAMs while circling over Tskhinvali and attacking columns on the ground (although there is another version of the story, in which it was shot down by a Russian fighter patrolling the area). The pilot successfully bailed out and, albeit wounded, eventually managed to reach his own ground forces.

In the same afternoon, a pair of Su-25s, again drawn from the 368th ShAP, mounted an attack against Marneuli airfield, the main Georgian jet base, located some 11nm (20km) south of the capital Tbilisi. The Frogfoots, which operated virtually unopposed – no SAM launches and AAA fire has been reported against them during the raid – used 80mm rockets to destroy three An-2 light transports.

In the morning hours of the second day, 9 August, the 368th ShAP continued its unsung and rather dangerous CAS work at low level and, before long, the regiment reported its second loss. This time the downed pilot was Col Sergey Kobilash himself; he was performing a mission south of Tskhinvali when his Su-25SM took a hit from a shoulder-launched missile. The aircraft, however, remained flyable for a period and Col Kobilash tried his best to return the damaged Su-25SM to base with the port engine inoperative. This, however, turned out to be a mission impossible, when the slow-flying Frogfoot took another SAM hit over the southern part of the Tskhinvali and the pilot had nothing to do but eject. After an uneventful parachute landing in the middle of a Georgian village near the city, Col Kobilash had the good fortune to be promptly recovered by a CSAR party.

This is the result of the close-proximity detonation of an Igla hand-held SAM during the August 2008 war in South Ossetia. This particular Su-25K, subsequently withdrawn from use, belonged to the 461th ShAP, an attack regiment stationed at the time at Krasnodar, and was flown by Maj S. Konukhov. (Author's collection)

The second Frogfoot loss in the same day, and the third in the war, occurred in the late afternoon of 8 August. It was the leader aircraft of a pair from the 368th ShAP, tasked to escort a Russian motorized column advancing from the Roki tunnel towards Dzahava and Tskhinvali. According to the wingman's accounts, the Frogfoot pair was erroneously intercepted by two RuAF MiG-29s (as the fighter pilots thought that they had engaged Georgian Su-25s) and immediately began defensive manoeuvring. While performing the scissors manoeuvre, the wingman, Capt Sergey Sapilin, recalled that the leading Su-25 was hit by a missile, supposedly fired by a SAM system in the forward hemisphere. The pilot, Maj Vladimir Edamenkov, failed to eject from the uncontrollable aircraft and was killed.

All three downed Su-25s and most, if not all, of the damaged Frogfoots were believed to have been hit by friendly fire, either by Russian land forces or by South Ossetian irregulars.

On 9 August, another Su-25-equipped regiment, the 461st ShAP, home-based at Krasnodar, joined the battle. It ended the war without losses, reporting only one Su-25K heavily damaged by a shoulder-launched SAM, but it eventually managed to return to the base.

By the outbreak of the war, the Georgian Air Force had an attack aircraft fleet comprising ten Su-25s. Four of these were upgraded to the Su-25KM Scorpion standard by Elbit Systems of Israel, while a further four were the non-upgraded Su-25 version, in addition to two two-seaters on strength. The only accounted operation by the Georgian Frogfoots took place in the early morning of 8 August, when six aircraft were prepared to bomb the 58th Army armoured columns that were slowly advancing towards the battlefield in Tskhinvali. In the event, only four Frogfoots managed to take off and deliver their ordnance on the enemy near the city of Dzhava, though all the 550lb (250kg) free-fall bombs that were dropped were said to have missed their intended targets. As a result, no losses were apparently inflicted on the Russian troops or equipment attacked. This fact has also been confirmed by Russian journalists who were travelling with the column that was bombed by the Georgians. There were Russian witnesses of another strike mission that was said to have been performed by a GeAF Frogfoot on 10 August against Russian forces and on an important bridge in the village of Gufta, though this specific mission was not confirmed by the Georgian side.

Two four-ship flights of Russian Air Force Frogfoots seen releasing FAB-500ShN retarded bombs from level flight – a preferred way of destroying area targets with a total of 32 high-explosive 1,100lb bombs. (Andrey Zinchuk)

Export Frogfoots in combat

The war between Iran and Iraq was the second local conflict of the 1980s in which the Su-25 proved it could fight and that it was an effective CAS machine. The Iraqi Air Force acquired as many as 69 single-seaters and four two-seaters in 1986–87, enough to equip two ground attack regiments. The Frogfoot saw extensive use in the closing stage of the war, again demonstrating an admirable degree of battlefield survivability. On one occasion an Su-25 was even said to have survived a hit by a MIM-23 Hawk SAM missile and, despite the heavy damage incurred by the powerful warhead, it managed to land.

The Iraqi Su-25s, however, were not used in anger during the 1991 war, and the only reported flying activity encompassed the escape of nine aircraft to Iran, two of which were shot down by USAF F-15Cs on 6 February 1991. A number of Iraqi Frogfoots were also destroyed on the ground during the coalition air strikes, with at least one example caught in the open at Jalileh airfield, while others were destroyed inside their underground shelters with bunker-busting Paveway laser-guided bombs.

This Iraqi Air Force Su-25K was destroyed during *Desert Storm* in 1991, caught in the open at Jalileh airfield. (SSgt Dean Wagner/USAF)

The small numbers of surviving Iraqi Su-25s were buried under the sand at several air bases on the eve of Operation *Iraqi Freedom* in March 2003; this way the Frogfoot did not represent any real threat to the coalition forces during their push towards Baghdad to overthrow Saddam Hussein.

The Angolan air arm was another early Su-25 operator that used its Frogfoots in anger in the 2000s. A total of 12 single-seaters and a pair of twin-seaters were delivered in early 1988, taken on strength with one squadron of the 26th Fighter-Bomber Regiment, stationed at Namib airfield. The Angolan aircrews began flying CAS sorties in late 1990, bombing the UNITA armed opposition forces, which advanced towards the capital Luanda. The type of combat missions performed by the Angolans, however, proved to be ill-suited to the Su-25, because they used it as a bomber, dropping its ordnance from 16,500 to 23,100ft (5,000 to 7,000m) in level flight. As could be guessed, this had very little effect – if any. As many as 25 combat sorties were flown in this war campaign and, by March 1991, the regiment had lost its combat capabilities.

Another local conflict where the type was used in anger was in Ethiopia, which in March 2000 took two former RuAF Su-25Ts, upgraded to the Su-25TK standard before delivery. These 'Super Frogfoots' were sold out together with a pair of second-hand two-seaters, upgraded to the Su-25UBK standard. One of these two-seaters was reported to have been written off in a landing accident in April or May 2000, probably at Debre Zeit air base near the Ethiopian capital of Addis Ababa.

Piloted by Ethiopian aircrew trained in Russia, the three surviving aircraft took part in the closing stage of the war against Eritrea, which ended on 10 June 2000. One Kh-29T TV-guided and two Kh-29L laser-guided missiles were reportedly used in combat, in addition to a number of S-24 240mm rockets. A total of 17 combat sorties were amassed in three weeks of fighting. It was the only instance of successful Su-25T export, after a decade of fruitless international marketing efforts, that was eventually revealed by Sukhoi Shturmovics's president and designer general, Vladimir Babak. He noted that Su-25TK pilots from a hot-climate export operator – undisclosed by Babak at the time – had mastered the employment of laser-guided missiles and successfully employed these in combat.

F   **A PERUVIAN AIR FORCE Su-25 INTERCEPTING DRUG-TRAFFICKERS**
Peru took delivery of 18 ex-Belarusian machines in 1998 – including ten single-seaters and eight two-seaters – and these saw use in anger in an innovative role as interceptors of drug-carrying aircraft. The Peruvian Frogfoots were rushed into action to undertake intercepts of general aviation aircraft smuggling raw cocaine and cocaine paste from the Upper Hulanga Valley in the northern part of Peru to neighbouring Columbia. The first shoot-down undertaken by the Su-25s in this new role was claimed in mid-2000 in an area north of the capital Lima.

A modern-day Su-25 pilot patch from the only NATO country still using the Frogfoot – Bulgaria.

The fledgling air arm of Macedonia took delivery of three ex-Ukrainian Su-25s and one Su-25UB two-seater (originally sourced from Belarus) in June 2001, under an urgent procurement programme. The newly acquired Su-25s were immediately used in anger, with Ukrainian mercenary pilots in the cockpit against the ethnic Albanian insurgents. There, the Frogfoots were reported to have been used in anger in a single mission, performing attacks using mainly 57mm rockets against a main battle tank, hijacked by the insurgents. This tank hunting mission, however, ended with no result. In addition, during the conflict, the Frogfoots flew several visual reconnaissance and 'show-of-force' missions over the insurgent-held positions.

Against drug-trafficking planes

Peru took delivery of 18 ex-Belarusian Su-25s in 1998, including ten single-seaters and eight two-seaters, and, not long after, these saw use in anger in an innovative role, as drug-carrying aircraft interceptors. In 1999 and 2000, the Peruvian Frogfoots were rushed into action to reinforce the nation's anti-drug campaign. Real-world air-to-air operations (anti-drug patrolling) proved that the straight-winged aircraft with extensive high-lift devices sported remarkable low-speed agility. The Su-25 also boasted a good thrust-to-weight ratio, which, in turn, enabled it to easily undertake intercepts of general aviation aircraft smuggling raw cocaine and cocaine paste from the Upper Hulanga Valley in the northern part of Peru, neighbouring Colombia. There were some reports of shooting down the drug-carrying aircraft with R-60M short-range air-to-air missiles and possibly the powerful GSh-30 twin-barrel cannon – the first shoot-down was claimed in mid-2000 in an area north of the capital Lima.

The Democratic Republic of Congo received four factory-new Su-25s acquired from TAM in 1999–2000; these were used in anger in several missions during the internal conflict in the country, flown by mercenary pilots from the former Soviet republics. Other African nations known to have used in anger their newly delivered Frogfoot forces in the late 2000s and early 2010s were Sudan and Chad.

The air arm of Ivory Coast was another Frogfoot operator that gained notoriety in 2004, as its aircraft saw use in anger against the opposition forces. At least four aircraft, two of which were two-seaters, were procured from Belarus in 2004. The two-seaters, flown by mixed crews – one local pilot and one Belarusian mercenary – deployed to Yamoussoukro airfield in late October or early November 2004, and soon afterwards began making attacks against the anti-government forces in the town of Bouake. The first strikes were undertaken on 4 November and, two days later, they erroneously attacked a French military camp, using 57mm rockets. Nine French troops and an American visitor were killed, while 23 others were injured. As a consequence, on the same day, the two Su-25UBs were immediately destroyed on the tarmac of Yamoussoukro by French Special Forces in an act of revenge; the other two apparently shared the same fate, being destroyed inside their hangar at Abidjan Airport.

CONCLUSION

The small and robust Frogfoot can now justifiably claim to occupy a prominent position in the generation of combat aircraft that was fielded en masse in the former Soviet Union during the 1980s, and the type still forms the backbone of the Russian Air Force's attack capabilities, albeit in considerably reduced numbers. The somewhat ugly and often underrated attack aircraft gradually but indisputably emerged in the early 1990s as Russia's most useful and cost-effective combat jet, as its armed forces rapidly switched from their traditional cold war posture to one of internal policing, faced with growing unrest around the fringes of the former Soviet Union in the 1990s and 2000s.

The basic Su-25 has proved – just like its American counterpart A-10 – a fairly successful aircraft, remaining in service longer and performing better than originally expected. (Alexander Mladenov)

The faithful Frogfoot is slated to remain in service with most of the operators at least until 2020 and near-terms sales of both new and second-hand aircraft to new operators worldwide cannot be ruled out. There are also a good many little-used Su-25s still available for sale in the former Soviet states and East Europe.

The type's success has been proved by the developments since the early 2000s and especially by the upgrade and life-extension packages on offer, as well as the series of export sales; this eventually refuted the conclusion of some Western aerospace analysts, who maintained in the late 1990s that the first-generation Su-25 is effectively dead in its single-seat form. There is plenty of life remaining for the upgraded and refurbished Su-25SMs, while the greatly improved new-build two-seat derivative – expected to appear by 2015 at the earliest – is slated to continue into the next three decades as RuAF's principal attack and close air support workhorse.

FURTHER READING

Bedretdinov, Il'dar, *The Su-25 and its modifications* (2nd ed., in Russian), Bedretdinov i Ko (2002)

Burdin, Sergey, *Su-25 Attack Aircraft* (in Russian), Harvest (2001)

Lake, Jon, *Sukhoi Su-25 Frogfoot*, World Air Power Journal, Vol. 30, Aerospace Publishing Ltd (1997), p. 50–97

Kojemyakin, Andrey and Korotkov, Andrey *Su-25 Attack Aircraft – 30 Years In Service – Part I* (in Russian), Moskva (2012)

Markovskii, Victor and Prikhodchenko, Igor, *Su-25 Gratch Attack Aircraft. Armoured Il-2 Successor* (in Russian), Yauza (2011)

Mladenov, Alexander, *Su-25 Frogfoot Family – Development & Upgrades*, International Air Power Review, Vol. 7, AIRtime Publishing (2002), p. 26–35

Mladenov, Alexander, *Su-25 Flying Fortress*, AirForces Monthly (July 2009), Key Publishing (2009), p. 50–58

Mladenov, Alexander, *The South Ossetia War*, AirForces Monthly (January 2010), Key Publishing (2010), p. 64–70

Mladenov, Alexander, *Armoured Workhorse*, AirForces Monthly (January 2013), Key Publishing (2013), p. 74–80

INDEX

Note: Page locators in **bold** refer to plates and illustrations.

abandonment of attack aircraft 5
aerial attack methods **51**, 53, **53**
Afghanistan war theatre 14, 43–54, **E46–47**
aircraft 5, **7**, 8
  Ilyushin Il-2 attack aircraft 5, 8
  Ilyushin Il-10 attack aircraft **4**, **8**
  Ilyushin Il-40 attack aircraft 5
  Ilyushin Il-42 attack aircraft **7**
  Mikoyan MiG-21 fighter 5, 16, 20
  Sukhoi Su-7B Fitter-A
    fighter-bomber 5
  Sukhoi Su-17M2 Fitter-D
    fighter-bomber 8
airframe and electric systems 19–20, 21
AOA (Angle of Attack limiter) 15
armour penetration 34, 38, 57
armour protection 6, **6**, **18**, **19**, 22–23, **23**, 29–30, 48, 52

Berzina, military exercise 5

carrier landing training 32
CAS (close air support) missions 4, 5, 14, **19**, 43, 44, 48, 53, 54, 56, 58
Chechen campaigns 56–57, **58**
cockpit construction 20, **20**, **29**, 29–30
combat survivability 22–23, **23**, 33, 50, 52–53
communication equipment 23, 37, 41

DASH (Display and Sight Helmet) 41
design and development 6–16, **7**, **15**, 30
dimensions **27**

export Frogfoots 28, **28**, 29, **C30–31**, 59–62, **60**, **F60–61**

FAB-500ShN bomb **27**, 59, **E46–47**
flare dispensers 50
formal commissioning of T8 15
fuel system 21–22
fuselage construction 18

Georgian Air Force, the 59
Grach (rook) **45**, 46, **57**
GSh-30 twin-barrel gun **26**, 34, 38, 46
guided missile strikes 49–50
Gulf Wars, the 59–60, **60**

HUD (head-up display) 37

Ilyushin, Vladimir 9, 10, 12, 14
Iran–Iraq war, the 59

Khod FLIR targeting system 36
Klyon-PS laser rangefinder system 27, 49–50
Kopyo radar 36
Koweta towed target 17

losses 46–48, **49**, 50–52, 53, 54, 58–59

'Mach buffeting' 12
maiden flights 4, **27**, **29**
ministerial decree for more powerful engine 10
missiles 36, 41
  9A4172 Vikhr 34, 35, **36**
  AIM-9L Sidewinder air-to-air **49**
  Kh-25ML air-to-surface 24, 38, 49, **54**, **B24–25**
  Kh-29L air-to-surface 26, 38, 49, 60, **B24–25**
  R-27R/ER & R77 36, **36**
  R-60 guided missile 24, 26, 40, **B24–25**
  Stinger hand-held SAM 51, **52**, **53**, **A11**, **E46**
move from analogue to digital 37
Multirole Modular Computer (MMRC) 41

navigation systems 23, 33, 34, 36, 37, 41, 45
need for new generation tactical strike aircraft 5–6
night combat sorties 50, 53

OGAB-100 & 250 bombs 46
operational use in post-Soviet era 55–56
Operation *Exam* 44–45
Operation *Romb* 4, 14, 43–44
operations map of Kandahar **50**
ordnance and munitions 23, 24–27, **26**, **27**, 33, 37–38, 42, 45–46, **B24–25**

Peruvian Frogfoots 62, **F60–61**
pilot patch **62**
post-Soviet Union fleet strength 55
pre-flight strengths 45
production 11, 14, 17, **19**, **27**, 32, 38
prototypes, T8 5–6, **7**, 8–16, **9**, **11**, **14**, 30, 32, 34–35, 43, **A12–13**

R-95Sh turbojet engine 10, 11, 12, 14–15, 21, **21**, 44
R-195 turbojet engine 16, 21, 35, 56
radar systems 36, 41, 42
rockets 10, 24–26, **B24–25**
  S-5 **44**, 45
  S-13T 38
  S-24 26, 46, 57, **B24–25**
RuAF (Russian Air Force) **17**, **33**, 35, **35**, 36, 37, 63
  IShAP (Instructor Attack Regiment)
    186th 17, 56
  see also VVS (Soviet Air Force)
Rutskoi, Lt. Col. Alexander **49**

SAMs (surface-to-air missiles) 50, 51, **52**, **53**, 58, **58**
self-protection systems *see* combat survivability
ski-jump trials 15, **30**, 32
South Ossetian War 57–59, **D38**
speed 8, **27**
Strepetov, Lt. Col. Grigoril **48**
Sukhoi, Pavel Osipovich 6, 8

Sukhoi Su-25 'Frogfoot' close air support aircraft **16**, **19**, **27**, 42–44, **51**, **54**, **63**, **A12–13**, **D38–39**, **E46–47**
  Su-25-1/UBM1 upgrade 42
  Su-25BM derivative 16, 17, **17**
  Su-25K 33, **58**
  Su-25K export version 28, **28**
  Su-25K export version A 28, **C30–31**
  Su-25K export version B 28, 59–60, **60**, 62, **F60–61**
  Su-25KM Scorpion 40–41, **41**, 59
  Su-25SM upgrade **37**, 37–40, **38**, 63
  Su-25SM3 upgrade 40
  Su-25T (T8M) Super Frogfoot **33**, 33–35, 36, 56, 57
  Su-25TM **35**, 36, **36**, 37
  Su-25U two-seater derivative **C30–31**
  Su-25UB 30, 41–42
  Su-25UB two-seater derivative (T8-UB) 28–30, **29**, 32, 33, **C30–31**
  Su-25UBK 29, 60, **C30–31**
  Su-25UT (Su-28) unarmed two-seater 30, 32
  Su-25UTG 32
Sukhoi versions never built 33
Suppression of Enemy Air Defence (SEAD) 41–42

T8 Project, the *see* prototypes, T8
tailplane installation 11
targeting systems 27, 34, 36, 49–50
technical specifications 18–21, **20**, **21**, **27**
testing 9–12, **14**, 14–16, **16**, 16–17, 32, 34–36, 40, 43
three-seat trainer aircraft 33
towed targeting 17, **17**
training 10, 28, **30**, 32
transition to high-altitude operations 53, 54

undercarriage construction 19
upgraded versions **37**, 37–42, **38**, **41**, 63

Vitebsk-25 self-protection system 40
VVS (Soviet Air Force) 5, 9, 10, 35, 55, **55**
  OShAE (Independent Attack Squadrons)
    200th 44, **45**, 46, 48
  OShAP (Independent Attack Aviation Regiments) 51, 55
    80th 17, 43, 44, 51, 55
    368th **37**, 51
    376th **50**
    378th 30, 48, **48**, 49, **49**, 50, 51, 53
  ShAP (aviation attack regiments)
    368th 38, 57, 58
    461st 28, 59, **D38–39**
  see also RuAF (Russian Air Force)

weapons *see* ordnance and munitions
wing construction 18
wing disintegration defect 14

Zvezda K-36L ejection seat 20, 23, **23**